Shooting Straight

A GUIDE TO ARCHERY EQUIPMENT

John Holden

The Crowood Press

First published in 1987 by
THE CROWOOD PRESS
Ramsbury, Marlborough
Wiltshire SN8 2HE

© Ocean Publishing 1987

British Library Cataloguing in Publication Data

Holden, John
    Shooting Straight: A Guide to Archery
    Equipment.
    1. Archery – Equipment and supplies
    I. Title
    799.3'2'028   GV1185
    ISBN 1–85223–010–X

Typeset by Inforum Ltd
Printed in Great Britain

Contents

Introduction

Data collected at tournaments and in the hunting world highlights a disturbing pattern. Over 90 per cent of beginners give up within three years of first drawing a bow, mostly because they cannot come to terms with their lack of progress. They don't expect to be world record holders or even county champions, but neither can they accept that, after trying hard, they are still unable to shoot accurately enough to enjoy themselves. Each lesson, practice session and tournament ends in a sense of failure. Every archer has a personal goal in mind – on average around 1000 for a FITA round, or hitting the vital spot of a deer at 20 yards – and if he fails to make that grade within a realistic period, he will almost certainly quit: usually in frustration, sometimes in disgust.

Nobody should make excuses for losing points or missing game due to bad technique or carelessness. When it comes to the crunch, the skill of the man behind the bow is what counts. No matter how sophisticated archery equipment becomes, that will remain true, and there is nothing to be gained by believing otherwise. But the questions still arise: are you achieving the rewards you deserve, or are you actually shooting much better than the results suggest? Are bow and arrow blurring your talents to some degree or perhaps even destroying them? How often do you prepare and execute a perfectly competent shot that might well have been a gold under ideal circumstances, but was actually a blue, black or even grass? Does the dream of venison evaporate when your broadhead buries in a tree and a scared deer disappears into the distance? How often do you shake your head and wonder what on earth went wrong that time?

CONTROL OR EQUIPMENT

Over the years authorities on archery have switched more and more emphasis to technique, insisting that modern bows, arrows and accessories are so advanced and reliable that nobody gains an advantage from equipment alone. Skill is the name of the game: if you want to get ahead, concentrate 100 per cent of your time and talent on learning how to shoot. Don't worry about stabilisation, tuning, and testing different arrows until you can pump out steady 1200-plus FITAs. For now, get a bow of the right draw weight, arrows of the right length and spined according to the chart, and start shooting. Later on, of course, you'll need to spend a lot of time tuning, but everyone has to do that: achieving perfect results is a very tricky business.

The archer is never entirely convinced by this approach. He begins with a fairly basic outfit, and for about a year channels all his efforts into learning the mechanics of drawing, holding and letting go. The results speak for themselves: within a few weeks all his shots hit the target; a little later a grouping pattern emerges. When twelve months are up, he is shooting around 3rd Class scores under the British Grand National Archery Society's (GNAS) classification system. On the FITA outdoor round this is roughly 600 points for recurve and fingers, and 700 for unlimited compound (approximately 500 and 600 points respectively for the women's round).

5

'High-tech' though it is, the compound bow won't shoot straight unless it is properly adjusted and matched to the arrows.

At this stage, most archers look at the expensive outfits used by the champions, kitted out with V-bars, extending sights and a set of X7's, and conclude that they would gain a lot more points by investing in something more sophisticated than their own basic tackle. So they take the plunge and after another year ot two of hard practice reach a level somewhere between 2nd and 1st Class on the GNAS table: 800–975 men's FITA with recurve, 900–1075 compound (women's scores are 700–950 and 850–1075 respectively). Then progress grinds to a halt; they either plod along at a similar level for the rest of their days or stop shooting altogether. They conclude that since they have worked hard and invested in the best of equipment, they obviously lack the skill, talent or whatever it is that makes a top-class archer – so why bother struggling?

EQUIPMENT SURVEY

The data that follows is based on observations made and questions asked over a three year period involving over a thousand archers drawn from a group who labelled themselves 'ordinary' or 'Mr Average'. All nursed the same desires: to shoot scores they could be happy with, or to hunt competently, within their limitations and the time available. All but a few were frustrated in their endeavour, and many were resigned to fail-

Skill, confidence and good equipment – *that's the winning formula.*

ing. Ordinary archers were chosen deliberately on the basis that it would have been pointless to survey the champions. The big problems in archery are not at the top of the tree, but in the roots. Look there to find the answers also.

Factors taken into consideration included how long the archer has been shooting, how much he practised, whether he had been formally coached or had picked up the threads as he went along. Bow make and model, draw weight and arrow specification were also investigated. In all, a vast amount of personal and technical information was gathered and collated. Even before a quarter of the survey had been completed, two significant findings emerged. By the end, they absolutely dominated the picture:

1. In at least 75 per cent of cases, there was no indisputable relationship between an archer's shooting *expertise* and his *results*. Many whose style and control seemed likely to approach or even exceed Master Bowman standard turned in appalling groups and consequently scores that by no stretch of the imagination reflected their potential. Even among those who were noticeably lacking in overall skill, or whose control was erratic, there was still a distinct imbalance between effort and reward.

2. Over 85 per cent of the equipment surveyed showed fundamental errors in set-up and tuning serious enough to prevent maximum accuracy and in many cases to completely rule out tight, consistent grouping. The pattern held true regardless of quality

Question or Observation	% Yes	% No	% Not sure
Are you absolutely sure that your bow is the right draw weight for you personally?	64	30	6
Are your arrows cut to optimum length?	40	15	45
Observation: brace height within maker's recommended range.	73	22	(5 – no data)
Do you know exactly what the brace height should be for you personally?	12	88	
Do you make your own strings?	32	68	
Observation: adequate string, serving and nocking point quality.	51	49	
Is your nocking point set by impact tuning point or similar test?	37	60	3
Observation: nocking point obviously wrong.	55	43	(2 – no data)
Are you happy with your stabiliser system?	26	71	3
Did you choose it after testing the other options available?	15	80	5
Or by copying somebody?	74	19	7
Are you satisfied that your bow is in tune?	23	61	16
Observation: pressure button set on or very close to bow centre (usually unstable).	58	38	(4 – no data)
Observation: obviously erratic arrow flight.	46	54	
Are your arrows selected on the basis of actual shooting and tuning results?	21	75	4
Have you ever investigated the possible benefits of stiffer shafts?	9	90	1
Do you check your arrows regularly for straightness etc?	86	14	
Do you clock them as well?	4	96	

and price; on average high performance bows were worse, probably due to their greater sensitivity to set-up and tuning.

Coupled to other statistics and implications drawn from the overall survey, these two vitally important areas confirm what many average archers have suspected for years but usually never dared mention for fear of being ridiculed by their peers, champions and coaches: namely, there *is* something wrong with the outfit; it *isn't all* the archer's own fault. The first part of this observation is certainly true: not only does Mr Average's score fail to reflect his true abilities, but all too often his bow and arrows rule out success of any kind. But the second part is definitely wrong: it is entirely his own fault. Mr Average's outfit (hunting or target, recurve or compound) is a very strange beast indeed. Based largely on a mixture of copying, myth, imagination and wishful thinking, it is rather like the horse designed by a committee – it turned out to be a camel. Worse than that, it is a badly built camel. However, there is a vitally important point to consider here. The quality and inherent performance of the items individually is not the problem. The fault is in how they were chosen, assembled and tuned.

Conclusions

At least 75 per cent of target archers and hunters are struggling under a severe technical handicap. It is probable that everyone falls into the trap early in their archery career. Perhaps this is inevitable; in some ways it may actually be a desirable step on the road to mastering the sport. If nothing else, getting into trouble does underline the importance of maintaining a balanced attitude towards equipment. A real tragedy is that only the lucky few ever escape.

Role of Equipment

The lesson to be learned is that there soon comes a point in the development of technique and control when the role of equipment must be carefully considered. Many archers know every scrap of technical information about various makes of bows, arrows and accessories. Everyone with a year or two's experience has a working knowledge of how to tune. But very few know anything about matching a bow to its stabilisers, sight and string, or how to choose the right arrow.

When experts say that equipment is not a very important factor in success, they mean that understanding such technicalities as carbonfibre limb construction and handle cross-sectional shape is of no direct consequence to an archer's performance. In engineering terms, one model of recurve or compound is very much like the rest, consequently little is

Bows may look similar, but their performance and suitability for the archer in question can be very different.

gained by comparing stored energy figures, deflex angles and velocity ratings.

In two respects, however, equipment is absolutely critical. Firstly, it must suit the archer's personal requirements – and not just the obvious ones like draw weight and length. Handle pressure point, for example, is so fundamental to accuracy that it can never be compromised. Secondly, every item from the bow itself down to the shaft nock must match each other *and* the archer. Only when style, control level, bow, arrow, string and accessories are in basic harmony can the outfit be tuned properly.

There is a popular misconception that the tuning process *produces* that essential balance between the archer and his equipment. It

Does your equipment give the results you really deserve?

The moment of truth!

cannot. A bow that does not suit the man, an arrow that fights the limbs' energy output or a string that planes from side to side under acceleration are impossible to correct on the pressure button, by altering the brace height or any other tuning trick. Real tuning is the simple, predictable process of adding a final sparkle of accuracy and stability to an outfit that is already working very nicely. If the bow suits the archer, the arrow and string match the bow, and the stabilisers react kindly to release and follow-through, there is very little need for adjustment. A tweak of the button, a few twists on the string, and a slight change in V-bar angle are enough to gel the entire system into a perfect shooting machine.

Tuneability is therefore an important symptom in the self-diagnosis of an archer's problems, especially relevant if he already has more than a suspicion that the bow and arrow are fighting him. Some aspects of tuning do demand time and no little effort: discovering exact brace height, preferred string diameter and stabiliser settings, for example. But the fine-tuning process – nocking height, centre-shot, button pressure and compound tiller – should be quick and easy. If not, this, coupled to any doubts already in the back of your mind, strongly suggests that you should start looking for the answers elsewhere in the equipment world, starting with the basics.

1 Compound or Recurve

Bow technology is now so advanced that there is very little to choose between most makes and models. Gone are the days of yew, lemon wood or even early fibreglass, when limbs or handle might snap after only a few months and no two bows ever shot identically. If the next man's bow was better than yours, he might beat you by a mile even though his technique was inferior. Today, everyone who enters a tournament or goes hunting with bow and arrows is on a much more equal footing – assuming that the outfit is correctly matched, set-up and tuned. Even the gap in performance between cheap and expensive bows is closing rapidly, eliminating yet another route for the archer determined to buy his way up the ladder if necessary. One backlash of such radical changes in the archery world is confusion about which bow to shoot. Which is the most accurate bow available? Is it worth spending £500 on a tournament recurve? Are compounds considerably more accurate and powerful?

For millions of archers, a compound is *the*

Recurves still dominate the tournament shooting line.

bow to own – a view reinforced by the weapon's 'high-tech' appearance and the greater control and accuracy it offers the ordinary archer. Despite what some experts say about the relative performances of recurves and compounds, it is a fact that armed with some basic instructions Mr Average shoots a lot more accurately and consistently with a compound. Moreover, he learns much more quickly – an extremely important factor in bowhunting because many participants are hunters first and archers second, having no particular desire to spend weeks or years perfecting one small aspect of their sport. The compound's dominance of hunting spills over to target shooting. In field shooting and hunting-related events like silhouette shooting it has already made the recurve virtually obsolete in some cases. Again, the underlying reason is the compound's comparative ease of control and enhanced accuracy for Mr Average.

FITA TARGET SHOOTING

Although the compound is officially sanctioned for use in FITA target archery, it has yet to make a significant impact. In some countries, the formal approach to target shooting that FITA represents is unpopular anyway. Archers who shoot compounds see no real need to compete, especially if they are already involved in more relaxed hunting-related and non-FITA field events. In countries like Great Britain where hunting is banned, compounds and recurves are more evenly balanced, though with an increasing bias towards the compound for field events of all kinds. The compound's influence on FITA and GNAS target events is also growing, but considerably more slowly. Indeed, it seems unlikely that any significant breakthrough will occur in the foreseeable future.

FITA events, indoors and out, highlight the confusion in archers' minds about the relative merits of each bow. A closer look at what actually happens when an archer changes from recurve to compound is the easiest way to clear up most of the questions. A bad archer gains nothing by switching; if he uses a release aid and scope sight he might well get much worse. The reasonably competent archer – shooting, say, 1000 FITA with recurve – could pick up 50–250 points depending on his technique and control.

Usually the score improves because the compound system irons out or sidesteps an ingrained fault which prevented the archer from shooting better with the recurve: a release aid would take care of some problems in the draw fingers and arm, for example. But there is a world of difference between raising scores and raising skills. The archer's real ability to shoot usually stays roughly the same. He is deceiving himself if he seriously imagines that by switching bows he has closed the gap between him and the recurve champions.

Comparisons can be made at virtually any standard of shooting, but are most interesting – and particularly significant – in one area. A recurve score of 1153 is equivalent to a handicap of 34, also known as Master Bowman (MB) level in the British GNAS handicap system. An unlimited compound MB handicap is 27, an FITA of 1223. Recurve archers of approximately MB standard who change to compound usually settle in at 1200–1250 FITA after two or three years with the new equipment; a big increase in points but no improvement in real terms, still being roughly MB standard. No doubt they gained a great deal of personal satisfaction from using the new bow and shooting tighter groups, but actually they are no more competitive. What often hurts is that the top recurve archers are still ahead – slightly in

A compound bow and release aid may bypass problems in the archer's draw arm and fingers . . .

points, vastly in skill.

The champions already shoot amazingly tight groups with recurves and fingers, and they lack neither technique nor control. The compound would iron out minor inconsistencies of style that result in the occasional arrow straying from the group, and it probably does have a tiny edge in ultimate performance which will increase as bows and arrows become more sophisticated. At the moment, though, very little is to be gained. With 30 and 50 metre world records already near maximum, where is the scope for making huge leaps? Leeway exists for improvement at 70 and 90 metres, but when wind and weather are taken into account scores probably would not rise dramatically. From the competitive angle, unless everyone used a compound there would be no point in making the switch anyway. The champions understand full well that when it comes to the crunch the best archers always have won and they always will. That is one reason why they became champions. Juggling the scores with different equipment holds no real challenge for them.

THE PERSONAL CHOICE

The compound bow has become first choice for hunting because it offers an excellent combination of easy handling, accuracy and high energy output which allows the new-

. . . but they cannot compensate for poor control and lack of back tension.

comer and less experienced archer to hunt safely and humanely after only a few weeks of practice and familiarisation. The same level of competence might take years to achieve with a recurve and longer still with a longbow.

In the target and field shooting world, choice is not quite so clear-cut. If you prefer to shoot good groups relatively easily with the most sophisticated bow yet invented, again the compound should be first on the list. The best place to learn and compete is among archers of similar outlook, which in most countries means joining a field club or bowhunter league. As already discussed, there is no challenge or satisfaction in competing against archers using bare bow or

freestyle recurve, or any other equipment completely different from your own.

At present, and for the immediate future at least, archers seriously intent on making the grade in FITA target competition must choose the recurve. There is no other way to meet the world's best target archers in direct competition until the selection committees and organisers of the World Target Championships and the Olympic Games allow compound teams to shoot side by side with the recurves. The question of status also arises: almost without exception, the world's best compound archers are professional and therefore would not be eligible to shoot under current regulations. Until both bows are catered for and professionals are permit-

Making it to the top in FITA target archery means shooting a recurve.

ted to shoot, the compound is unlikely to achieve the status and recognition it deserves. Consequently, frustration and sometimes friction will continue at all levels, even down to club and county tournaments.

The only real solution for compound shooters is to beat the recurve archers at the highest level, thus establishing the bow's superiority once and for all. The day that happens, there will be the revolution in target archery that compound enthusiasts and manufacturers dream about. Until then, the committed competitor is likely to stick with a recurve – and this has to be the best advice for the beginner as well.

GENERAL SELECTION FACTORS

Quality and Performance

Engineering and design standards are surprisingly high throughout the enormous range of bows available today. Discounting some very cheap Far Eastern recurves and 'toy' compounds, variations in arrow speed and accuracy are fairly small; certainly, you don't get twice the performance by spending double the money. On the other hand, quality control seems to be higher on the more expensive bows, and they do offer a much wider range of lengths, draw weights and tuning facilities. If you are particularly tall, short, strong or weak, or have an unusual style, these factors in the accuracy equation might only be available on the most advanced, expensive models. If physique and technique are average, a much cheaper bow might shoot equally well and last just as long. Compound or recurve archer, you can spend a fortune without gaining a single point and sometimes your performance will drop.

The natural tendency is for the choice of

Excellent quality can never be cheap due to the craftsmanship and handiwork involved.

bow to be influenced or even dictated by external pressures: advertising, endorsement by a leading archer or what the club champion uses. Bows are so evenly matched these days that this is not necessarily a mistake unless the archer also copies his hero's draw weight, arrow length and stabiliser system on the same theme. The overwhelming priority is to use an outfit that suits him personally. If common-sense guidelines are adhered to, in all probability a bow of any make in the middle-upper price range will perform adequately. Arrow speeds, sight settings and tuneability may differ a little, but the on-target results are broadly similar. Today's bows – even the recurves – are inherently more accurate and consistent than even the world champions can exploit.

Another way of looking at it is that many cheap target compounds and take-down tournament recurves are more than capable of shooting 1250-plus FITA, a performance achieved consistently by only a handful of international archers.

Personal Preference

Any objective comparison of bows ignores the vital areas of feel, confidence and personal preference which do make substantial differences to performance. Consider three top tournament recurves: Hoyt GM, Marksman Portland 2000 and Perris Whitehart. On paper there is nothing to choose between them in speed, stability and accuracy. They are all equally well built. The Hoyt has the advantage of vertical arrow rest and limb tiller adjustment, plus an unequalled reputation. The Whitehart and Portland 2000 are more basic in design, much less expensive and although they lack world-wide recognition are nevertheless of superb quality. A good archer can shoot well with any of them, but he shoots best with one. Exactly which depends on those indefinable subjective qualities that add up to a feeling of rightness and preference. The Hoyt would suit many archers, in which case the money is well spent. To others the Portland or Whitehart would feel much better and as a result produce higher scores.

If you ask any successful archer of world

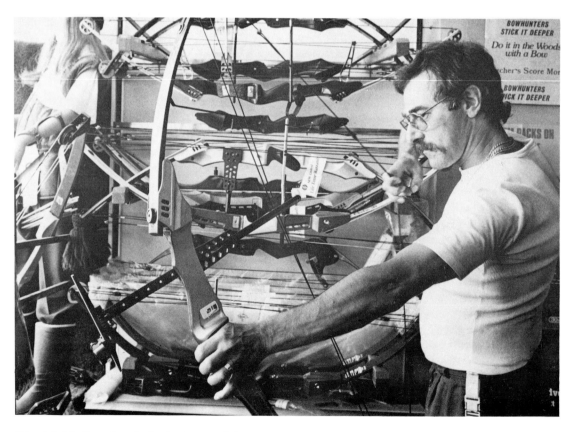

The right 'feel' to a bow is absolutely essential.

or national level why he shoots a particular bow, you might be disappointed by the lack of technical reasoning. Rather than praise its draw-force characteristics, carbon limbs or advanced stabiliser system, he might simply say: 'I like the feel, and I'm confident about shooting with it.' A few cynical observers might add 'And, of course, he's being spon- sored by the manufacturer as well.' True, but might this not add to its appeal? On the other hand, nobody ever became world champion or even a strong contender with- out shooting a bow he really believed in. Archers further down the tree would be well advised to choose their bows on similar prin- ciples.

2 Bows

COMPOUNDS

Round Wheel or Cam

Round wheel or cam type, the compound bow's great advantages over the recurve are reduced holding weight at full draw, followed by a smoother injection of stored energy into the nock during and after release.

Lower vibration, greater stability, compactness of design and reduced limb flexure are further bonuses which contribute to easier shooting and sometimes to greater accuracy as well.

During the first part of the draw, the poundage of a regular wheel compound builds up fairly gradually to peak weight, which is maintained only briefly as the

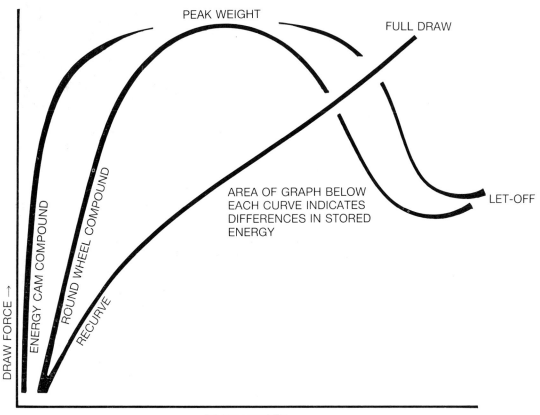

Draw force characteristics.

wheels revolve towards their let-off position. Poundage then falls until the wheels exert maximum leverage as full draw approaches. The let-off (reduction in draw weight) is now about 50 per cent of peak weight, and the draw is described as being 'in the valley', a reference to the characteristic dip in the draw-force graph curve. Pulling further generates a rapid increase in draw weight because there is no more free movement in the cables. This is called 'pulling against the stops', and is for most archers the ideal full draw position because it helps maintain good back tension. The bow also stores more energy and gives slightly higher arrow speeds. All the same, the main advantage is to improve the hold, make the draw length more consistent and give a cleaner, crisper release.

The obvious way to increase a compound's stored energy is by holding peak weight longer, which is achieved by altering the shape of the wheels into eccentric profiles called energy cams. For any given draw length, an increased dwell at peak weight can only be achieved by reducing the build up and steepening the fall off into the valley. Consequently, a cam bow feels much stiffer and is more tiring to draw because the weight builds up quickly and holds longer. Late in the draw – disconcertingly so for many archers – it suddenly plunges into the valley.

On release, the string hits the arrow nock much more viciously than on a wheel bow, boosting paradox and increasing the bow's sensitivity to poor set-up, tuning and technique. Even shot with the release aid, the sudden acceleration and prolonged peak loading gives far less latitude. To compensate for that, the shaft must be stiffer than that which could be shot perfectly from a wheel compound of equal poundage whose energy output pattern is so progressive and gentle that paradox is virtually eliminated when a release aid is used.

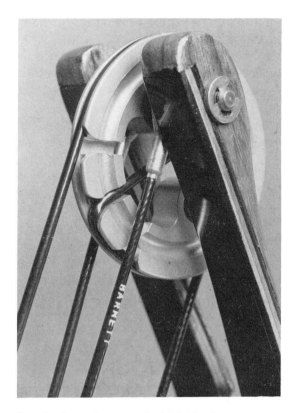

Standard round compound wheels blend smoothness and control with high performance.

Because the speed of a compound bow is basically the result of its ability to shoot light arrows (the efficiency of a compound and its stored energy figures are nowhere near so superior to a good recurve as many archers imagine), energy cams are sometimes self-defeating in velocity terms due to the stiffer, heavier arrows required, especially for finger release. However, the let-off at full draw, along with the greater steadiness and control it offers Mr Average, certainly gives the cam bow an advantage over a recurve of equivalent draw weight.

All things being equal, the higher the performance of a bow, the harder it is to tune and shoot. 'Hot' cams are notoriously difficult to handle and may well result in less accuracy and lower arrow performance because so much energy is wasted. They are manageable only when shooting a heavy, stiff shaft. The problem is aggravated if the archer uses an overdraw device. As a result, many experienced hunters and nearly every serious tournament archer prefer either a mild cam action or ordinary wheels. Control and accuracy are much better and the bow is easier to set up and tune. High efficiency and better transfer of energy to the arrow are guaranteed, so velocity and kinetic energy are close to, and sometimes better than, that which can be extracted from a 'nervous' cam bow of the same peak weight.

The less competent the archer and the lighter his arrow, the nastier a cam bow becomes. For this reason alone it makes sense for a beginner to choose a round wheel model at first. Sometimes even the experts find cam bows too hard to handle and simply not worth the effort. The worst combination of all is an inept archer, a high-performance cam bow, overdraw and ultra-light arrows chosen with velocity specifically in mind.

Bow Length

As with recurves, the length of a compound affects its performance and stability, though rarely to the same degree. A distance of 46–49in between axles gives an ideal combination of speed, balance and ease of shooting. Shorter bows tend to be faster and slightly more convenient to carry in the field,

A long compound gives extra stability under tournament pressures.

but they usually impose a penalty in harshness and forgiveness and are sometimes noisier as well. Compared to recurves, length is not nearly so important for clean release. Finger shooters enjoy the comfort afforded by the low holding weight which allows the string to run nicely around the fingers instead of pinching them against the arrow nock.

Limb Construction

Standard and economy models are usually fitted with solid glassfibre or glass/carbon limbs, which generally give good performance. Limb shape is nowhere near as critical in a compound as it is in a recurve, because the limb flexes little between brace height and full draw. Some materials are more efficient than others in how they store and release energy, but the big influence on arrow performance is limb weight.

Light limbs accelerate more quickly and accurately, transfer more energy to the arrow and therefore shoot quietly and without excessive shock. Whether this really matters in hunting and all-round tournament work is open to dispute, especially when arrows are used that make the bow run efficiently. A heavy, stiff arrow absorbs a high proportion of the limb's energy, leaving very little to show up as vibration and harshness. Under hunting conditions there is little, if any, practical difference in accuracy and performance between good quality solid limbs and the laminated kind. Ultimately, though, laminated limbs do offer a margin of performance that cannot be equalled by any solid material currently available. Lighter, more precise and with superior energy storage and release characteristics, they add that special something which separates the very best bows from the rest. Excellent tournament archers gain accuracy, control,

tuneability and forgiveness. Mr Average might be hard pressed to detect any difference in scores and groups, but he will certainly appreciate the more refined feel and reaction when the bow is drawn and shot.

Draw Length and Poundage

The compound's adjustment for poundage and draw length encourages a relaxed approach to bow selection. The standard 10–15lb range of draw weight and plus or minus one inch on draw length seem to provide more than enough leeway for final specification and tuneability. But there are definite hazards in this approach. The bow's peak weight varies according to the position of the cables in the wheels or cams. Reduce the draw length and you also lose poundage. Increase the draw and the poundage rises. There are also changes in stored energy and bow efficiency.

Within reason, the preferred peak weight can be restored by adjusting the limb bolts, but seldom without affecting bow stability or even safety. Raising poundage by screwing in the limb bolts alters the deflex angle between limb and handle, which in turn destroys some of the bow's basic shooting stability; the amount depends on the bow's design and tuning. Backing off the bolts to reduce poundage deepens the triangle formed by the handle pressure points and the limb axles. The immediate effects on shooting stability are small, but in the long term problems may arise due to the excessive gap between the limb base and the handle. Vibration and noise tend to increase, but the real danger is sudden and dramatic limb or bolt failure at full draw; for this reason alone, manufacturers usually specify how far the bolts may be loosened.

Wherever possible correct draw length should be achieved with the cables in the

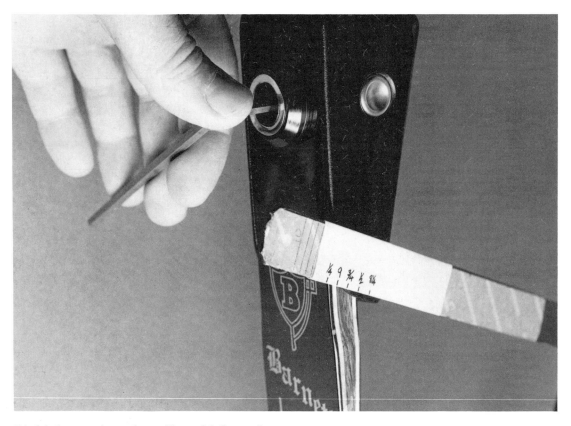

Limb bolts control poundage, tiller and deflex angle.

standard mid-position on the wheels or cams. The poundage figures of most compounds are based on that setting and are seldom maintained when the cables are fitted into the longer and shorter slots. An archer shooting 27in arrows on a 27–29in bow nominally rated 50–60lb would get little more than 55lb at peak setting. Another drawing 29in might not get down to 50lb without risking damage to limbs, bolts or handle bushings.

Despite AMO and other technical guidelines, the working draw length of a compound bow is more variable than on a recurve. First, you need to know whether the manufacturer measures draw length to the valley of the draw-force curve or to the stops. Next, you must personally decide where to draw: in the valley, hard against the stops or

some point between. The only way to match the bow to your style is by actually drawing it. Even then there are risks. Most archers unfamiliar with a compound initially overdraw due to the let-off, a tendency exaggerated by a release aid and peep sight.

The draw weight specification of the bow should also be chosen so that the actual poundage required falls in the lower half of the range where the bow is generally more stable and pleasant to shoot. For example, an archer who wants to draw 50lb would generally do better to choose a 50–60lb model than one of 40–50lb. However, due to the wide variation in wheel and limb design, brace height, draw-force pattern and arrow specification, this is by no means an infallible rule. Expert guidance pays dividends; if you

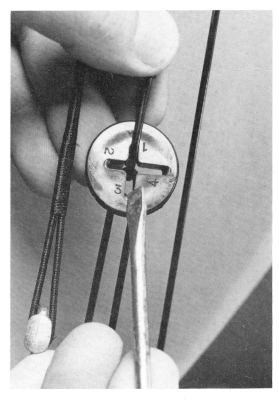

Compound wheels must be synchronised. Barnett's adjuster irons out small imperfections in roll-over.

can shoot the bows beforehand, so much the better.

RECURVES

After centuries of development, the recurve bow has probably reached its peak. Its accuracy and power are excellent due to advanced limb design and modern materials. Stability and tuneability leave little scope for improvement because bow geometry and design are now so well researched and understood. Indeed, it was the recurve's limitations that prompted the invention of compound bows. An inevitable spin-off from the pioneering work by Hoyt, Yamaha and

Marksman in particular is that virtually every aspect of recurve design is common knowledge. Some bows from the Far East are blatant copies of previous Yamaha and Hoyt recurve models that between them rewrote the record books at World and Olympic level. Sometimes the performance of the look-alikes is not quite as good due to inferior fibreglass laminations and lower engineering tolerances, but in general the shooting differences are very small.

More good news for target archers is that top quality limb materials are freely available on the open market, which enables small specialist bowyers to compete extremely successfully with the industry's giants. There is every reason to believe that as the compound continues to make inroads into the mass archery world, the best tournament recurves will eventually become the domain of the master craftsman rather than the assembly line worker.

The quality and performance of all well-known makes of recurve can be taken for granted, and there should never be difficulty in finding the correct poundage and draw length. The archer is thus free to concentrate on how the bow feels and how it reacts to his style and degree of control – a highly personal approach enhanced by the confidence of knowing that whatever make and model of bow he eventually does select, its accuracy, reliability and stability will be of the highest order. After all, there is nothing worse than finding a bow you really like only to discover, too late perhaps, that it is difficult to tune and exaggerates every tiny shooting error. For example, it may not be cut far enough past centre to shoot the arrows you like; or the width of the grip may not suit your hand. Despite the generally high standard of quality control in the middle-upper end of the recurve market, checking the new bow beforehand for defects is nothing less than common sense.

The Perris Whitehart built by Tony Preston is a classic example of specialist bowyery.

Handle and Limb Alignment

The most common complaint from archers concerns the straightness of handles and limbs. Properly die-cast or sand-cast, an alloy handle should be accurate enough to satisfy the most fussy of archers. Now and again, a twisted handle manages to sneak through the quality control department; occasionally one or both of a pair of limbs shows a similar fault. It is hard to judge exactly how much a bow must be out of alignment to affect accuracy and performance, but the archer's confidence is seriously undermined – how can he trust a bow that looks like a banana?

Unless a handle meets with an accident after it leaves the factory, bend or twist is probably due to stress patterns in the metal. Most alloys used in bow making take a permanent set within a few days of being cast, after which little or nothing can be done about it. This raises two important points for the archer. First, never trust a dealer who offers to correct the fault. It is virtually impossible to do so without destroying the metal's temper and strength; replacement is the only answer. Second, because the fault will be present before the bow arrives at the shop, it is a wise precaution to inspect the handle before purchase. Stand about six feet behind the strung bow and align the string with the limbs. It should pass straight down the centre of both and cut through the coun-

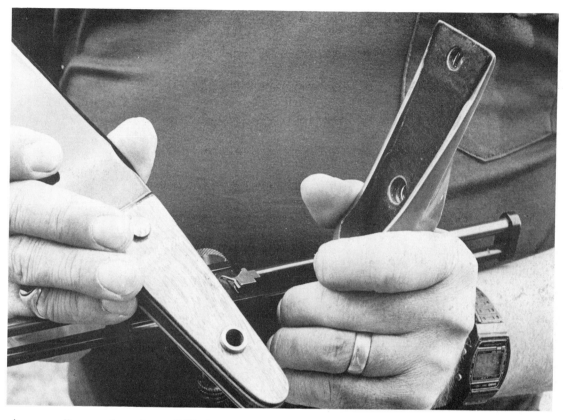

Accurate alignment depends on solid limb attachment.

terweight bushing on the handle. Also check that the string sits neatly in the limb tip grooves. If the bow is bent, substitute another handle or pair of limbs to see exactly where the fault lies.

Be careful not to confuse a genuine limb fault with bad stringing technique. Even perfect limb tips and grooves do not automatically align with the string and handle when a bow is assembled. Often a small adjustment of the recurve is required to make the string seat properly, and unless this step is taken before shooting the limb might well take a set. If the bow is left strung in this fashion for a long time, the twist will become permanent and eventually harm the laminations as well as reducing performance. On the other hand, if twist cannot be instantly

and permanently removed from a new pair of limbs, perhaps they are already faulty. Above all, beware of the helpful archer or dealer who says he can straighten them with heat!

Centre Shot

Most take-down handles are cut so deeply past centre that an arrow can be aligned exactly on the string/limb mid-line yet still leave plenty of clearance between the shaft and the bow window. Others are only slightly over-cut and must be shot with the arrow lying well left of centre. There is no reason to think that a deep cut-out is necessarily better. For one thing, few archers can tune and shoot properly with the arrow set

Proper stringing protects the recurves from twisting and unequal stress.

exactly on centre anyway. Generally it should be angled slightly left of the bow's mid-line; offset by about a shaft's width at the tip when string, arrow and bow limbs are eyed up from six feet behind the bow. Most bows including those with a limited cut-out give adequate window clearance at that setting, so it can be argued that extra cut-out is wasted. However, a great deal depends on the archer's choice of shafts.

If the archer prefers arrows stiffer than recommended by the Easton matrix, he might well need to set the pressure button closer to bow centre (though still slightly left of exact centre-shot), in which case some handles would not give enough clearance. On average, British and European take-downs have about $\frac{1}{8}$in less leeway than American and Japanese bows. Owing to the strength and design factors involved, wooden-handled take-downs and one-piece hunting bows are difficult to manufacture with a deep cut-out, making clearance and tuning slightly more difficult.

Bow Length

Bow length is not usually critical, but this does not mean it can be left to chance. For any given draw length and poundage, a short bow is faster, less stable and tends to pinch the fingers, while a long one is slower, steadier and more comfortable. As a rule a long bow is the better option, but there are pitfalls. Unless a bow is drawn far enough, its limb recurves do not work properly; consequently, power and accuracy are lost. Shooting 27in arrows from a 70in bow, for example, would lead to poor sight settings, difficult tuning and low grouping power. At the other extreme, pulling 30in arrows on a 64in tournament take-down would overwhelm its limbs, leading to stacking, pinched fingers and highly unstable arrow launch.

All leading manufacturers give specific recommendations for matching their bows to the archer's draw length and required poundage. There are also specific recommendations for handle and limb lengths individually. Some archers need a long limb and short handle, while others shoot much better with a bow of the same length but with a long handle and short limbs. The manufacturer's technical information is extremely important because it bypasses many of the strange theories that abound among archers and some dealers. Even so it is essential to shoot the various combinations before making a decision. A chronograph is invaluable, because in this particular aspect of bow design arrow velocity is a sound basis for compari-

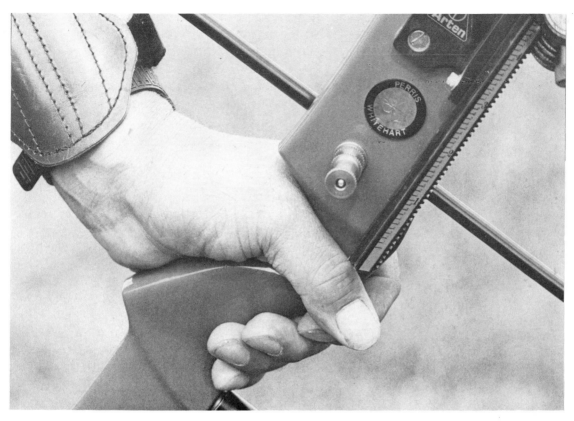

Handle length, shape and centre shot may affect arrow selection.

sons. The handle/limb configuration giving the highest, most consistent velocity rating usually offers the best balance between performance, stability and control.

Tiller and Poundage Adjustments

The perpendicular distance from the string to the base of a recurve's limbs is usually smaller on the lower limb, by around ⅛–¼in on average. The measurement reflects the tiller of the bow, which in simple terms describes the balance between the individual energy storage and output pattern of each limb. A recurve does not shoot properly if its limbs are identical in strength or deflex angle (the angle at which they emerge from the handle). The real problem is that the arrow rest and shaft nock are not positioned halfway up the bow and string. To counteract this vertical imbalance and other factors including handle pressure point and draw finger position, the two limbs must be rebalanced dynamically by either building the lower limb stiffer and/or altering its deflex angle.

Tiller, deflex angle, the shape of the limb recurves and bracing height are so closely interrelated that a bow cannot give its best performance unless every angle and pressure is carefully controlled. Although an adjustable bow gives scope within this framework for extra tuning, nothing ever happens in isolation. To adjust one setting is to affect them all. The question is, do the benefits justify the drawbacks? Increasing the draw

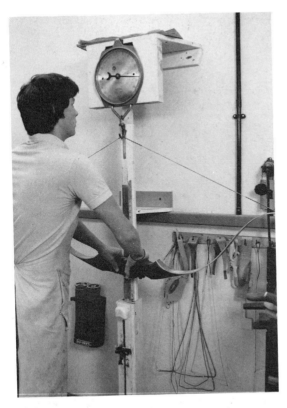

Some leading bowyers still insist that poundage and tiller should be set permanently by the factory.

manufacturers, dismiss the adjustment facilities out of hand. It is obviously not a clear-cut issue, and no doubt the arguments will continue until the case is proven one way or the other. For the moment, the archer who does not own the latest in adjustable bows can take comfort from knowing that, at most, he is at only a tiny disadvantage.

Hand Grips

Although champion archers disagree about many aspects of equipment and technique, they are united about the importance of the bow's hand grip. Many of them would reject a bow regardless of its reputation and performance unless the grip was absolutely right or could be modified to suit the shape of their hands. By contrast, hand grip is the last point that most less able archers would think about. If the one supplied with the bow did not feel right, they would happily learn to live with it.

Comfort is high on the list of priorities, but it must be considered alongside pressure point and torque control. Any grip that generates high torque and/or puts the pressure line through the wrong part of the hand or handle is disastrous no matter how good it feels, and must be weeded out without delay. Sometimes another grip from the range available for the bow eliminates these technical problems, in which case there is a good chance that it will also feel comfortable. After all, comfort is closely allied to relaxation, which in turn is of paramount importance in setting up the correct foundation for accuracy and control.

If the right interchangeable grip is unavailable, an existing one can usually be modified to fit. High spots are shaved down, low areas built up with a resin based filler like Isopon P38. Within reason, the shape and size of a grip are not particularly critical

weight may add a few feet per second but it must also decrease brace height and alter limb deflex angle, both of which promote instability.

Only the archer himself can answer these questions, but he should never approach the matter without considering that in the majority of cases the advantages are minimal whereas the potential for destroying some aspect of performance and control is at best considerable and at worst inevitable. However, given the required skill and experience a few archers do find the exercise well worthwhile and the extra cost of such sophisticated bows more than justified. Other equally competent but perhaps more cynical archers, along with some major

Choose a comfortable grip that feeds pressure correctly into the bow handle.

provided that two design points are not violated:

1. Hand pressure should feed straight into the back of the handle to minimise torque.
2. The grip pressure point must remain vertically below the button and at the distance beneath originally specified. The performance and stability of older bows could be improved by altering this vertical gap between pivot area and button – sometimes called the set position – but on modern takedowns it is precisely calculated and rarely can be changed by even a fraction of an inch without reducing performance and stability.

Draw Force Curve and Bow Efficiency

A graph of poundage plotted against draw length shows some interesting differences between recurve performances, and in particular it allows a surprisingly accurate preview of how the bow feels to draw and shoot. To plot the graph, measure the draw weight in one-inch increments from brace height to about three inches past full draw. Construct the curve by pegging the draw length along the horizontal edge of the paper and the poundage along the vertical.

Some older-style American and European bows – and many of the current low priced Far Eastern copies based on them – show a fairly even balance of weight and length all the way to full draw, around which poundage begins to increase disproportionately. The curve indicates good basic design within the limitations of the limb materials, but with a tendency to stack (that is, suddenly to feel harsh and solid). A modern, high quality bow of the same draw weight gives a quicker build-up just beyond bracing height, settles down in the middle of the curve and maintains its smoothness well beyond full draw position. The characteristic feel during the draw is initial stiffness followed by a silky build-up all the way through the clicker. Bow geometry and superior materials provide this valuable edge in control and reaction; and although the draw weight is the same as on the older models, the stored energy figure is higher, which usually means that the bow shoots faster and gives better sight settings.

Stored energy is represented by the area under the draw-force curve. The easy way to calculate it is by listing the poundage achieved at each one-inch step of draw (beginning one inch past brace height and stopping at the archer's full draw length), totall-

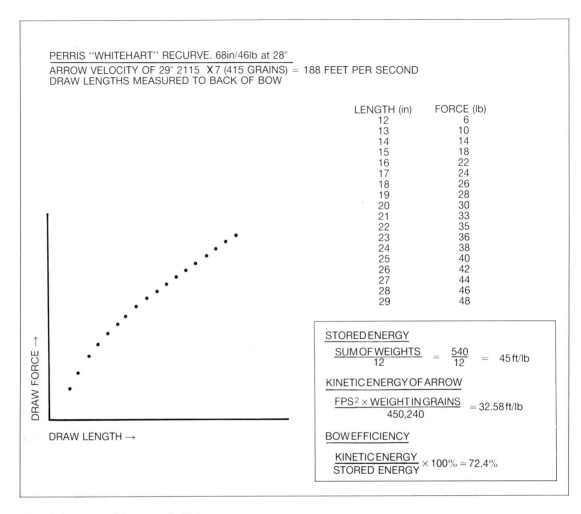

PERRIS "WHITEHART" RECURVE. 68in/46lb at 28"
ARROW VELOCITY OF 29" 2115 **X** 7 (415 GRAINS) = 188 FEET PER SECOND
DRAW LENGTHS MEASURED TO BACK OF BOW

LENGTH (in)	FORCE (lb)
12	6
13	10
14	14
15	18
16	22
17	24
18	26
19	28
20	30
21	33
22	35
23	36
24	38
25	40
26	42
27	44
28	46
29	48

DRAW FORCE →

DRAW LENGTH →

STORED ENERGY

$$\frac{\text{SUM OF WEIGHTS}}{12} = \frac{540}{12} = 45\,\text{ft/lb}$$

KINETIC ENERGY OF ARROW

$$\frac{\text{FPS}^2 \times \text{WEIGHT IN GRAINS}}{450,240} = 32.58\,\text{ft/lb}$$

BOW EFFICIENCY

$$\frac{\text{KINETIC ENERGY}}{\text{STORED ENERGY}} \times 100\% = 72.4\%$$

Draw force, stored energy and efficiency.

ing the weights and dividing by twelve. The answer is stored energy expressed in foot-pounds. Useful in itself, it is also used to determine the efficiency of the bow/arrow combination.

The difference between the stored energy and the arrow's kinetic energy (*see* Chapter 7) reflects losses within the system due to all manner of things from tuning and technique to static hysteresis (mechanical 'stickiness' and inertia) in the bow itself. To calculate a bow's efficiency, divide kinetic energy by stored energy and multiply the result by one hundred to reach the percentage. The figure applies to one set-up specifically and will always change in step with arrow weight, style, tuning and virtually everything else that can be varied. All things being equal, the higher the result the better. Around 75 per cent is a respectable figure for most bows, including compounds. Less than 70 per cent indicates too much energy going to waste – which will inevitably show up as noise, vibration and erratic arrow flight – while the high 70s reflect current limitations in bow design.

3 Bow Strings

'You must be content to put your trust in honest stringers. And surely stringers ought more diligently to be looked upon by the officers than either bowyer or fletcher, because they may deceive a simple man the more easily. An ill string breaketh many a good bow, nor no other thing half so many. In war, if a string break the man be lost, and is no man, for his weapon is gone . . . and therefore God send us good stringers both for war and peace.'

Thus Roger Ascham stresses the importance of the bow string in his book *Toxophilus*, first published in 1545. He goes on to discuss the effect of a string's length and construction on bow performance. The words are as true in today's world of carbonfibre and Kevlar as they were when, 200 years before Ascham himself, Edward III's longbowmen slaughtered the French at the Battle of Crécy. Yet throughout history, archers have underestimated the string's vital role in good shooting. To quote Ascham again: 'A thing though it

String performance is critical and highly personal.

be little, yet not a little to be regarded.'

At the most obvious level, the string is simply the means of transferring the archer's muscle power into the bow limbs, then to the arrow. The implication is that the bow controls the string, but the opposite is nearer the truth. Between them, string and arrow virtually dictate the result of the shot. No matter how perfect the archer, no matter how good his bow and arrow, the string has an enormous effect on speed and accuracy, smoothness and ease of shooting.

The AMO string specifications laid down for bow length and draw weight do not necessarily guarantee the best possible results. The string will be safe, reasonably long lasting and of a length that conforms with the bow manufacturer's requirements. So far as many archers are concerned, that is all there is to say about a bow string. Attitudes are very different at the higher levels of target shooting though: weight, number of twists, exact brace height (plus or minus $\frac{1}{8}$in is considered a wide variation), serving materials, string roundness and consistent strand tension are considered critical factors in achieving pin-point accuracy. Strings are therefore such a personal matter that serious archers prefer to make their own or have them custom-made by somebody they trust. AMO approved or not, mass-produced strings are not in the same class.

The extent to which the average target archer or hunter should insist on the finest string depends on his objectives and on how well he shoots. Most people would be happy to know that their strings detract nothing from their skill. Unfortunately, it does not necessarily follow that even a good quality commercially made string will therefore be good enough for Mr Average.

STRING SURVEY

Six Dacron and six Kevlar strings were bought at random for a well-known make of recurve target bow. Three of each were from the bow manufacturer; the rest came from various commercial string makers. Two strings, including one from the bow manufacturer, were outside the AMO tolerances. The rest were inside, but still required significantly different numbers of twists to achieve the right brace height, in this case $8\frac{3}{4}$in to the button.

Completely free from twists, the shortest string would not come within $\frac{1}{2}$in of the maximum brace height of $9\frac{1}{4}$in recommended for the bow. To reach the lower limit of $8\frac{1}{4}$in, the longest had to be twisted so hard that it distorted. An experienced archer would reject these two rogues, but a novice would probably be happy to fit either because they are still more or less in keeping with the overall bracing range of the bow. He would assume, as many do, that it is sufficient to stay somewhere within the suggested figures. The idea of a precise brace height seldom occurs to an archer until he shoots well enough to detect the difference that even $\frac{1}{4}$in can make.

String	A	B
Normal	—	4in
1	6in	5in
2	12in	8in
3	7in	5in
4	5in	4in
5	Too erratic to measure	
6	8in	8in

The first shooting test took that relaxed approach to string height into account. One after another the strings were fitted without

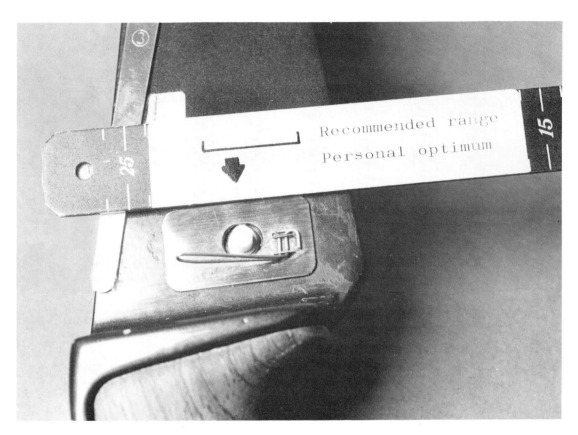

Tight groups depend on establishing the exact string height for the archer and his arrows.

adjusting their length and shot without tuning or checking. Two were smooth, three were noisy, the longest was noisy and rough. Group diameters at 30 metres are shown in column A of the table. Next, each string was adjusted to 8¾in or as close as possible. Most were fairly smooth and quiet, and these results are shown in column B. A custom-made string normally used on the bow was shot for comparison.

Diameters quoted are for the main group. Obvious floaters were disregarded in measuring, though it is highly significant that the worse the group, the more floaters there were. String 5 was so erratic that no recognisable group pattern emerged after 24 shots, so the test was abandoned. The huge

variation in group sizes spells inconsistent tournament results: the archer in question averages 330–335 points for 36 arrows at 30 metres on the 80cm face, but on the basis of these results he could suddenly drop under 250, apparently without explanation. String 5 might even convince him that he had completely lost the ability to shoot.

Anyone who does not know exactly which string best suits his shooting inevitably loses control and accuracy somewhere along the line. Smooth, quiet shooting is no test of a string's performance. Sometimes a bow sounds and feels beautiful but turns in terrible groups. Others are noisy and a little harsh when perfectly tuned. Probably *the* symptom that archers should be aware of is a sudden

35

change in scores and/or sight settings when a string is replaced. The only way to identify and correct the situation is by experiment. No technical aspect of archery is more vital than an understanding of bow string construction and tuning. Anyone committed to shooting high scores is at a serious disadvantage if he leaves such an important area to chance. He should know exactly what length, material, serving, number of strands and twists, brace height and nocking position ensure the best results.

DACRON OR KEVLAR

Kevlar's minimal stretch – about 2–3 per cent compared to Dacron's 5–9 per cent – allows the bow's limbs to channel more energy to the arrow. The string itself is stable and consistent during that split second after release, far less variable than Dacron, promoting extra arrow speed, improved sight settings at long range and higher accuracy. But a Kevlar string lacks the cushioning effect of Dacron, is also much harder on the bow, and its life is lower due to the severe stress on the fibres. In the early days of Kevlar bow strings, limbs could easily be delaminated or would snap. Besides, to get the best from the material, brace height had to be lowered by at least a quarter of an inch to make the recurves work properly, but this probably increased the harshness and noise. Although ordinary archers wondered whether the risks justified the benefits, the vast majority of top class shooters were agreed that Kevlar opened the door to higher, more consistent scores.

Today, virtually all tournament recurves are not only robust enough to use Kevlar but are designed specifically for it. Limb construction and draw-force characteristics are so well matched to Kevlar's limited stretch

Kevlar fails dramatically – but after the arrow has been shot.

that the bow shoots nowhere near so well with the comparatively elastic Dacron. Despite this, many archers are still reluctant to switch from Dacron because they are nervous about Kevlar's life-span and expense. And isn't it dangerous as well, judging by those frequent explosions on the shooting line?

If Kevlar were to break at full draw, the risks might be higher. Such is the material's character, that except by some millions to one stroke of bad luck, the string will always snap after the arrow has left it. The vicious jolt as the limbs relax is an unnerving experience quite capable of destroying the archer's concentration and confidence, but nothing like as dangerous as some anti-Kevlar archers suggest. Of the handful of injuries reported, most were due to shooting Kevlar on an old bow. In the even rarer cases where a string broke at full draw with serious consequences, it is significant that Dacron was to blame.

String Life

Some archers are convinced that a string should see them through from one season to the next. When Kevlar snaps after about 1500 shots they regard the material as short-lived, unreliable and expensive. Almost all problems with Kevlar stem from this basic misconception. In reality, anyone who uses Kevlar should learn to treat his strings as disposable. However, the life of a good string shot from well-matched equipment is at least 1000 shots, and it might well be double this. To look at it another way, a string that does not last for at least 750 shots is definitely suspect in quality and specification.

Length, thickness and twists are the foundations of reliability and performance. Once those are correct, many of the so-called critical aspects like serving and lubricants are minor or may even be discounted. Despite recommendations to the contrary, a Kevlar string can be served with monofilament, does not need lubricating under the nocking point and can safely be folded for storage. Although absolutely even strand tension is desirable, it is far from essential.

The Stretch Factor

The amount of stretch in Kevlar is normally measured on raw filaments and is virtually nil. Elasticity increases slightly when the filaments are spun into bowstring thread, but still offers no protection from sudden shocks. In this respect Kevlar has direct parallels with flax and hemp, the natural yarns from which ropes and cords have been

Laid-in loops (right) may help to protect Kevlar fibres in a highly stressed string.

made for centuries. The secret of a rope's strength and resilience lies in its pattern of twists which confer a surprising degree of elasticity to the non-stretch raw material. The same principle is used to make a better Kevlar string, as by controlling the number of twists you can build in an exact amount of stretch, which in turn gives longer life and often a better shooting performance as well.

Depending on the number of twists, a Kevlar string can have a stretch factor approaching five per cent, at which the filaments are well shielded from impact shock and therefore last much longer than the untwisted string usually recommended. However, a certain amount of efficiency is lost and there is a greater risk that the threads will cut into each other. A more realistic

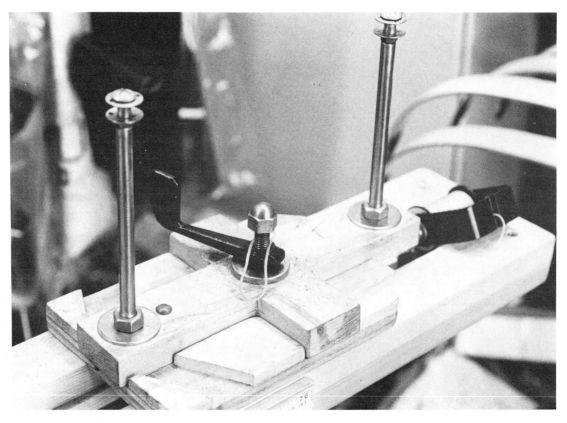

String making 1 *Jig design is unimportant provided that the pegs are
accurately placed and rigid. Otherwise, string length and strand tension
will vary.*

compromise is about three per cent elasticity, which gives at least 1000 shots plus a
substantial increase in bow performance over
Dacron.

There is no formula for calculating the
number of twists that best suit an individual
bow, nor is one necessary. Instead, make up
a set of three test strings. The first should
give the correct string height with just
enough twists to hold the strands together.
Make the second string $\frac{1}{4}$in longer than standard, and the third $\frac{1}{2}$in longer. Both must be
centre-served *after* twisting to the correct
bracing height.

Although they are of the same bracing
height, the strings will produce subtle

changes in feel, smoothness and bow reaction. Arrow speed and grouping may alter,
and almost certainly the bow will need tuning specifically for each string, though this
usually entails little more than a tweak on the
pressure button. After that, each string is
shot until it shows signs of deterioration or
actually breaks. (Worn twisted strings often
distort under the centre-serving, giving a
clear indication of internal damage long before they break.)

One or both of the twisted strings will not
only last longer than the standard, but will
shoot better as well. If the second string
offers a worthwhile improvement, the original untwisted string is only a little too

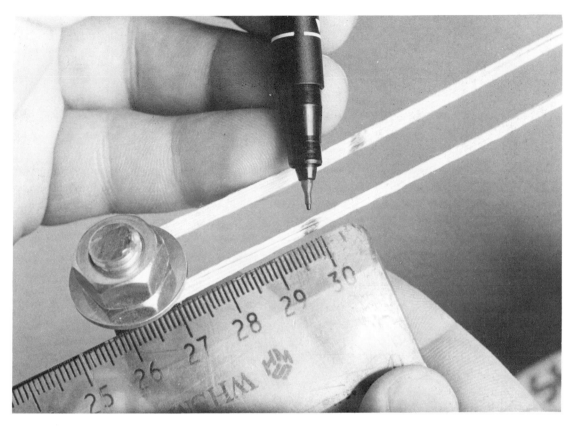

String making 2 *Mark the loop serving length, allowing about ½ in of overlap.*

vulnerable to stress; if the longest string gives better service, breaking strain must also be considered. All things being equal, this means that there are too few strands and/or the Kevlar is not of sufficiently high quality. About two twists per inch seem to produce good results on most target recurves, and this is therefore an ideal basis for experiment.

Diameter and Weight

A thin string is fast but sensitive and fragile. A thick one lasts longer and is easier to shoot, but reduces performance. As a rule of thumb, this makes sense; but applied to Kevlar does not necessarily hold true. A few

extra strands not only extend string life, especially in conjunction with a fair number of protective twists, but also enhance performance. It is generally recommended that a Kevlar string should have 50 per cent more strands than the equivalent Dacron string to guarantee adequate breaking strain, reasonable insurance against impact damage and roughly the same diameter. This leaves no latitude for error, especially in strand tension: every strand must work to full capacity, otherwise the string will snap prematurely. It is here that Kevlar is most vulnerable to less than perfect design and construction. The logical answer is to increase the number of strands, but this is traditionally rejected on the grounds of excessive string weight.

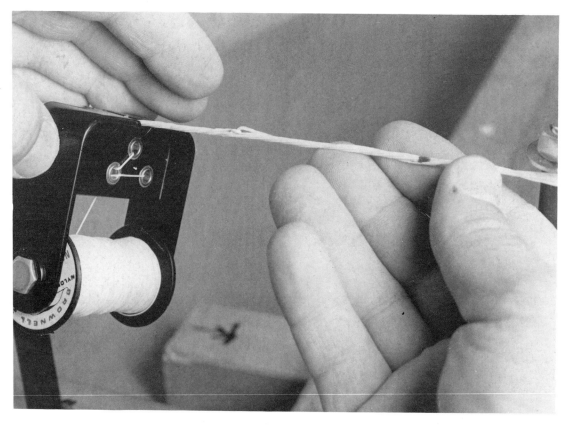

String making 3 *Serve evenly, with moderate tension.*

A thicker string is more comfortable to hold and release and is usually a better match to the arrow nock. The extra diameter is of no significance in terms of increased air resistance and planing; if anything, it is a shade more stable and forgiving. The very high breaking strain also helps counteract uneven strand tension. The slight extra weight rarely has a noticeable effect on arrow speed or limb performance. Every 100 grains added to the string makes the arrow perform as if it were about 25 grains heavier, so in practical terms the reduction in speed and sight settings is minimal or even undetectable in most cases. Depending on the original set-up and tuning, a heavier string might even enhance performance.

The risk of building up too much weight is reduced by unwaxed bowstring Kevlars. Marksman and Double E brands are gaining quite a reputation among archers of all levels. String diameter can be stepped up quite substantially without incurring a drop in performance. A thin coat of wax on the outside of the twisted string is sufficient to protect the surface from water, prevent fraying and also to hold the strands together when the string is off the bow. Standard non-stretch and special low stretch (about four per cent) versions are available. The 12 strands recommended for a 45lb recurve are as thick as 20 strands of other Kevlars, but the bow shoots at least as well and the string itself lasts far longer: up to 2000 shots is a reasonable expectation.

String making 4 *Swing the jig back to its starting position and continue serving for about 4in.*

Roundness and Stability

A string with a grossly oval or irregular cross-section does not leave the fingers as smoothly as a round one. It also tends to plane from side to side, paradox fashion, throughout the power stroke and thus affects the arrow. There is no evidence that minor imperfections have a measurable effect on groups; on the other hand there is no room for complacency either.

Endless loop strings with the strands neatly aligned, reasonably equal in tension and moderately twisted, produce the correct round cross-section almost automatically. Any slight imbalance can be resolved by rolling the braced string between two flat pieces of wood about six inches square,

paying special attention to the nock area. (The centre-serving should always be applied after the string is twisted to length and ironed smooth.) Laid-in strings require more care because the plaiting process characteristically produces a fairly pronounced spiral effect; bad strings look like twin cord electrical flex. The real solution is to take more care with the laying in of the strands, particularly when the second loop is plaited.

Serving and Nocking Point

The latest Kevlar materials are perfectly well served in twisted, braided or monofilament nylon. A meaty, unwaxed Kevlar string with plenty of twists does not actually need the protection of braided nylon, but, even so, it

String making 5 *Centre serving tension is adjusted so that the diameter matches the nock.*

is a very nice material to use. More comfortable to shoot than monofilament, and less prone to fraying than twisted nylon, braided nylon is highly recommended for its shooting qualities alone. The coils should follow the direction of the string, and the string itself should be twisted towards the bow window. Serving is more accurate and durable this way, and the string promotes slight pressure between arrow and rest during the early stages of release. For some archers this can be a critical aspect of tuning, so it is well worth experimenting with strings twisted in both the right and wrong ways. Sometimes the differences in group size and shooting consistency are remarkable.

A useful spin-off from the latest Kevlars is

a better relationship between string diameter and nock size. The 12 strands of Marksman thread recommended for a 45lb bow are ideal for the $\frac{9}{32}$in nocks most commonly used for this draw weight. Any minor adjustments are taken care of by serving thread tension. If the string is too thin (very few archers are troubled in the other direction) add extra strands to the whole string rather than pack out the nock area. Light, unwaxed Kevlars allow that option without reducing performance, not only making a neater job but also increasing the string's life and sometimes its performance as well. By the same token almost any nocking point system can be used, from dental floss to the latest plastic inserts. Compression damage should not be a

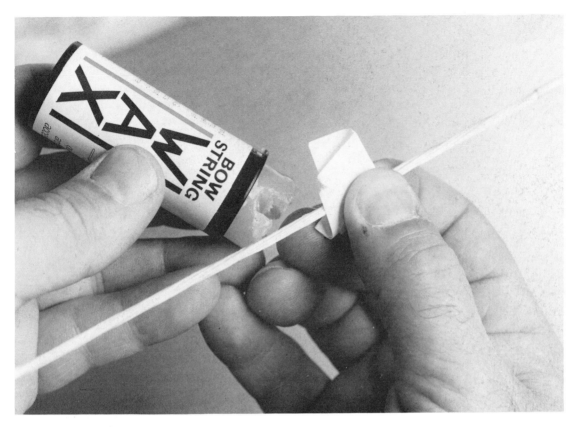

String making 6 *A surface coating of wax holds the strands together and protects the string from rain and dirt.*

problem even with crimped collars of the Nok Set design. Some archers lubricate the Kevlar under the nocking point with light silicon or machine oil to reduce abrasion. Whether this is strictly necessary is open to debate, but it certainly does no harm.

Hunting Recurves and Compounds

Hunting recurves are short and powerful, unforgiving of technique and rather harsh due to the limb geometry. Here, Kevlar offers no practical advantages over Dacron; in fact, a few trial shots with Kevlar are enough to convince anyone that in this case the old material is highly desirable. On the other hand, it is still important to find out which length, number of strands and twist pattern gives the best results. Just as much care should be taken with the string's construction, especially in retaining continuity of performance from string to string. Whereas it is easy to make two identical Kevlar strings, a pair of Dacrons call for much more attention to details like jig tension and consistent strand pressure. The only guaranteed method is to pre-stretch the Dacron for a day or two before winding it on to the jig.

Compound strings should· be made from Dacron because the high energy output and lack of shock absorption in the limbs and wheels themselves means that string stretch is a vital part of the system, without which

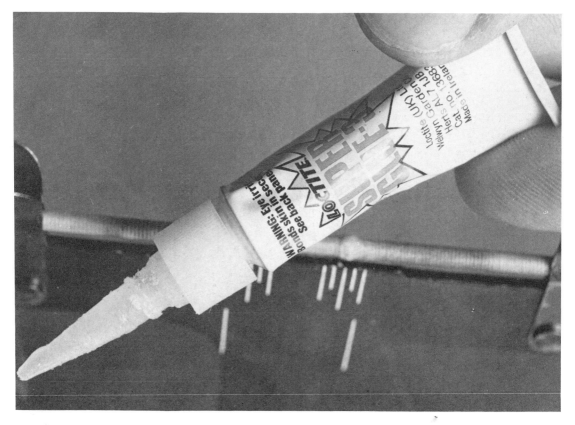

String making 7 *Cotton or dental floss soaked in Superglue makes durable, precise nocking points.*

the bow would shake itself apart. On top of that, there is no real advantage in Kevlar's unique characteristics anyway. Construction follows the normal theme except that a compound string should be twisted the bare minimum necessary to hold the strands together. Twist it more, and the cable pigtails will twist as well. String length should be that recommended by the bowyer. Longer strings are potentially hazardous because in extreme cases they could cause the cables to jump from their wheel grooves.

4 Stabilisation

Stabilisation is another subject that reflects the revolution in bow technology of the late 1960s, before which stabilisers were something of an optional extra, their use largely a matter of personal preference. Many excellent archers chose not to use them because the unadorned bow proved perfectly adequate even at world championship standards. In contrast, today's high quality tournament bows are designed specifically with stabilisers in mind, and by not using them the archer would lose shooting comfort, tuneability and grouping power. They are an integral part of the bow, not an optional accessory.

Stabilisers have a pronounced effect on the build-up of a shot, its release and the result. The mistake is to assume that this effect is always beneficial. A stabiliser system is equally capable of destroying accuracy and making life considerably harder for the archer himself. Even apparent short-term gains could backfire in the long run by masking errors which the archer would otherwise have identified and eradicated before they became ingrained habits. Good stabilisation therefore entails striking a balance between advantages and disadvantages, and it is not a subject to be taken lightly.

Bow stability involves centres of gravity, mass, inertia and leverage. Although it pays dividends to understand a few of the principles (for example, that a long rod with a small weight can have the same effect as a heavy weight on a short rod) selection and set-up lean far more towards abstract qualities like feel, smoothness and balance. The right subjective feedback from bow to archer generates confidence, which of all the factors in successful archery is universally accepted as being most valuable. For the majority of archers, the best system to use is simply the one they like best. Since the only way to discover it is by experience, there is no alternative but to try everything. It is not a particularly expensive or time-consuming project.

FADS AND IMITATION

Not having approached the subject with an open mind, many archers never arrive at the perfect system for them personally. The common trend is to copy the set-up used by world class competitors or even the club champion. Given that the vast majority of top archers use a V-bar system there is some logic in this, but it ignores the fact that stabiliser selection should always take account of the archer's level of skill. A V-bar does offer unrivalled freedom of feel and reaction and is probably a shade more accurate, but it also demands a high level of control and consistency from the archer himself; nothing is worse for exaggerating bad control and tuning.

Stabilisation must also be compatible with technique and physique. The perfect system for a tall, heavy archer using a style reliant on static tension cannot be expected to give similar results for a short, thin archer using a more dynamic method. The bow reacts differently in each case and its stabilisers must be chosen and arranged accordingly. With the many variables involved, it is quicker and safer to start from square one and develop your own personal set-up.

Good feel and reaction are priorities.

BUILDING BLOCKS

Old recurve bows were reasonably stable due to the weight of the riser plus the limbs' fairly low power output. Early attempts at increasing stability entailed adding extra weight directly to the top and bottom of the handle section. From this developed the twin stabiliser system which shifted the weight forward from the handle by means of short rods. Further gains in accuracy and balance were made by adding a third weight on a long rod to the middle of the handle, thus producing high inertia without imposing too much weight in hand. The overall effect of this 'flat' long rod/twin set-up was to counteract torque, reduce limb vibration and provide a more predictable, stable launching pad for

the arrow. Enhanced by TFC bushes and counterweights on the inside of the handle, the system is still used today even though it is sometimes regarded as inferior to more modern stabilisers. The real limitation of the long rod/twin arrangement is its pronounced weight-forward bias. Counterweights reduce the follow-through reaction, but sometimes make the bow awkwardly heavy.

Of all the stabilisers available, the flat system is by far the easiest to set up and shoot successfully. Like the long rod alone – another very useful but overlooked stepping-stone on the road to good stabilisation – it is highly tolerant of shooting style. While giving a fair degree of insurance against minor mistakes, it does not cover up more drastic errors such as unwanted bow arm tension or flinching. If anything, the forward bias helps the archer to spot them sooner. The bow also remains easy to tune and is nowhere near as critical of arrow specification and button adjustment as it may become when a V-bar is fitted.

As an introductory package, long rod and twins are highly recommended; archers who ignore them are missing an essential step in their education. A good plan is to start with the long rod only, add twins later, and finally counterweights if necessary. Many of today's tournament bows do not respond well to twins alone, so the long rod (about 30in with a 2–3oz weight) should always be the first step.

THE V-BAR SYSTEM

By improving balance and inertia around the handle pressure point and arrow rest the V-bar gives a slight boost in accuracy, but far more importantly allows great versatility in feel and reaction. Adjusting rod length, V-bar angle and weights, you can make the bow weight-forward, neutral or even back-heavy. Compared to the flat rod system, the reaction also seems dull. Some archers use the words 'alive' and 'dead' to describe the relative sensations during release and follow-through.

Before shooting a V-bar, an archer should understand the essential difference between it and a long rod/twin combination. The latter is inherently weight-forward in reaction and remains so almost regardless of rod length, weight and counterweight. This is the main reason why the system is easy to live with, making no special demands on technique or tuning. By contrast, a V-bar is highly critical of set-up. One extra weight on the long rod or a 20 degree shift in rod angle may have an enormous effect on shooting charac-

teristics and accuracy. It depends on the archer himself whether these changes are good or bad. The only way to learn about this 'Jekyll and Hyde' personality of the V-bar system is by experience, starting with the basics.

Bow Reaction Patterns

Some archers shoot best if the bow reacts positively during release; others do better with a static set-up where the bow hardly moves throughout the follow-through period. Experiencing and assessing these opposing reactions should be a priority because they are fundamental to the use of the V-bar system.

Begin with the long rod and V-bar itself (no short rods or weights). Check the brace height, nocking point and bare shaft planing pattern at about 15 yards. If necessary, re-tune the bow so that the bare shaft groups with the fletched shafts. There is no point in fine tuning at the moment. So far the reaction is moderately weight-forward due to the long rod.

Now screw in the V-bar rods and weights. In the horizontal plane (as seen from above the bow) the rods should be approximately at right angles to each other. Loosen the screws that control vertical adjustment until the rods swing free. Now you need an assistant: draw the bow and adjust the elevation so that the arrow lies parallel to the ground, then ask your assistant to tighten the V-bar screws. Gravity will have set the rod angle to vertical.

Shoot the bow and check its feel; for maximum sensory feedback, stand close to the target and shut your eyes. The reaction will be strongly weight-forward, perhaps disconcertingly so. Now alter the vertical rod angle by about 20 degrees towards the bow and shoot again. Although the reaction is still definitely weight-forward, giving a pro-

Key area 1 *Balance in hand during draw and hold.*

nounced jump forward and a vertical tilt, it is not so severe. Continue the test until the rods are parallel to the ground and inside the handle.

As the test progresses, you will notice that the bow continues to jump forward, but far less than before. As the rod angle alters, the top limb tips forward less and less during release until finally a state of neutrality develops during which the limbs and string remain virtually upright after the shot. The bow might now jump slightly upwards as well as forwards, though the vertical component is very small.

The third stage occurs when the V-bar weights are well inside the bow and approaching horizontal. The bow feels nice and steady during release and may even

jump forward a little. But the follow-through reaction feels wrong, with the bow toppling backwards and the long rod tilting above the sight line. The strength of reaction depends on the balance between long rod and V-bar weights, ranging from an almost imperceptible reverse bias to a severe backwards jerk of the top limb. In extreme cases the arrow will foul against the rest or bow handle. Although this final reaction is interesting to observe, the most important aspect of the test is to identify the three distinct phases of balance: weight-forward, neutrality and backwards. Backward reaction is never desirable and, once experienced, should be avoided.

A V-bar system adjusted for neutral balance produces slightly superior conditions

Key area 2 *Stability during release and arrow launch.*

Key area 3 *Controlled reaction in follow-through.*

around the arrow rest and pressure button, which in turn should promote better performance and accuracy. On the other hand, the bow also becomes more sensitive to the archer's style, reducing the margin for error or even proving to be totally incompatible. By contrast, the weight-forward design, although slightly less efficient in theory, more than compensates by being much easier to tune and shoot, Tolerant of most styles of shooting, it also has a considerable capacity to iron out minor errors and inconsistencies from shot to shot.

The wide variety of V-bar designs seen at Olympic and world level show that weight-forward and neutral balance each have their devotees and that many archers prefer a combination of the two. In every case, the exact format has been arrived at by experience and careful testing. The onus is on the archer to shoot the various options and discover which provides the best combination of feel, forgiveness and accuracy for him personally; when it comes to the crunch, there is no other way. As a rough starting point, midway between maximum weight-forward and neutrality gives good results for the majority of archers. With the short rods angled back at roughly 45 degrees – slightly behind the handle – the bow is close enough to neutrality to gain stability around the hand grip and arrow rest, but still weight-forward enough to cope with variety of styles and minor imperfections in style and tuning.

The theme can be taken a step further by raising the rods a little more to achieve true neutral reaction, then adding the necessary weight-forward bias by screwing an 8–10in rod and weight to the top bush of the handle. The extra inertia and leverage at this point also makes the bow more resistant to radial torque, and less sensitive around the pressure button. If there can be any such thing as a 'standard' V-bar set-up, this is it. However, the need to establish precise balance and reaction should never be ignored.

V-bar Variations

The pronounced nosedive of a heavily weight-forward V-bar system is reduced if the short rods are left to swing freely. Gravity holds them vertical while the bow is drawn and aimed, but when the handle and limbs punch forward after release the swinging weights lag behind, in effect dragging the bow's centre of gravity towards the inside of the handle. Brief though it is, this shift towards neutral balance enhances stability while the arrow clears the bow.

The horizontally flat arrangement where the short rods and V-bar are placed further forward of the handle by means of a 3–6in extension rod produces a good compromise between arrow rest/pressure button performance and the forgiveness of weight-forward balance. The weights on the horizontal short rods are nicely placed inside the handle geometry, but their fulcrum is outside and well forward. The system is stable and fairly easy to tune because like the old long rod/twins set-up, its moments of inertia are nicely placed around the vital pressure point/arrow rest area. Although the weights and rods can be selected to give a fairly neutral reaction, the system is essentially designed to be weight-forward. In practice, this means restricting how far the V-bar weights come inside the handle. Nor should they overwhelm the long rod: the bow

Extended V-bar.

should still punch and tilt forward during follow-through.

Rod Length and Weight

If you double the length of the rod, you generate twice the leverage and increase inertia fourfold. These laws of physics explain why a long rod is so effective in steadying the bow before and after the shot, and underline the need to be cautious about rod length and the amount of weight screwed to the end. Too much weight creates so much inertia than the bow's normal reactions are overwhelmed. High leverage does not help either; in extreme cases it prevents clean arrow launch by cranking the arrow rest or bow shelf into the shaft: 30in with 2–4oz is about right for most recurve bows. The 24–

Long rod and twins are a fairly lightweight combination popular with women.

26in option is a little too short for all but the lightest draw weights and arrow lengths, but is ideal for use on extended V-bar systems. Coupled to the 4–6in V-bar extender, this shorter rod holds the weight at just the right distance from the bow for optimum leverage and inertia with the standard 2–3oz weights provided. At the other extreme, 36in-plus rods are generally not recommended. Apart from anything else, the weight often obscures the target when the sight is set for long distances.

Twin rods follow much the same principle because they also stabilise the bow by exerting strong moments of inertia and moderate leverage. In the 30–45lb bow weight range, 8–10in rods usually prove satisfactory with weights of 2–5oz. The exact weight to use must always be determined by experiment, being as sensitive as a long rod to shooting technique, tuning and limb reaction. The real danger lies in excess weight which sometimes kills bow efficiency and accuracy. The rule of thumb is to use less weight if in doubt.

Bows are extremely sensitive to the weight, and to some extent the length, of V-bar rods. A length of 6–10in supporting 2–5oz suits most tournament recurves in the 35–45lb class. Excessive weight/length on the long rod calls for much more weight on the V-bar to produce the right balance in-hand and the desired reaction when the arrow accelerates. All-up stabiliser weight and size is an important consideration because, taken to extremes, the bow becomes so unyielding around the handle area that the shaft hits the rest or even the window. A bow *must* be free to react sideways slightly when the arrow passes the sight window. If it is not, fine tuning and clearance become extremely difficult and, worse still, the limbs cannot deliver full power.

TORQUE FLIGHT COMPENSATORS

Some archers consider the TFC to be a shock absorber pure and simple – a device inserted between bow and stabiliser to reduce or eliminate vibrations during release. Valuable though it is, this is only half the story. The real benefit of a TFC is control of stabiliser reaction time and damping power. If stabiliser and handle are linked rigidly, rod and weight exert their full influence from the moment the fingers begin to relax from the string. By detecting and absorbing small muscular and nervous reactions that occur a split second before the string is freed, the TFC could even be said to anticipate the event. Then as the arrow accelerates rapidly through its paradox cycle, the stabiliser maintains its restraining influence.

In one way this is an excellent state of affairs, but it also makes the bow more sensitive. By promoting excellent stability in line

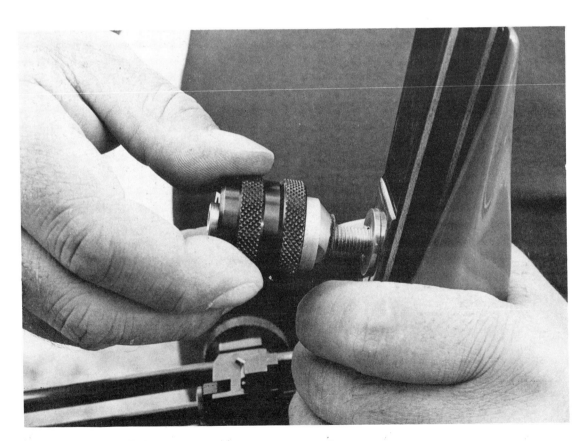

Torque flight compensator incorporated into the limb bolt.

with the target and by reducing the effect of handle torque, the long rod benefits from a rigid attachment. This explains firstly why a long rod should always be used without a TFC, and secondly why the damping power of carbonfibre is so useful in long rod design. By contrast, rigidity in V-bar rods and twins can easily result in lack of forgiveness if the length/weight of the rod generates too much resistance in the handle. A properly adjusted TFC not only gives a little slack in the system but also slows down the speed at which the stabilisers react. If the stabilisers themselves are well chosen and correctly positioned, TFC tension is not critical because there is already plenty of latitude in the system. Thus, the usual recommendation of setting the TFC to medium-high tension makes good sense. The rubber inserts provide a little insurance against mistakes.

If equipment is less than perfectly matched and therefore inherently difficult to tune, slackening the TFCs often improves results by allowing some extra 'give' in the handle, thus permitting cleaner arrow launch. On much the same theme, TFC adjustment sometimes allows heavy weights to be used for improved in-hand balance while the bow is drawn and aimed, yet reduces their stabilising effect by making them react more slowly and less powerfully. You get the benefits of improved centre of gravity without the penalty of enormous inertia that would otherwise interfere with arrow launch or even destroy limb performance. The degree of control depends on draw weight, stabiliser design, arrow length, tuning and technique – so many variables that only trial and error can reveal the benefits.

COMPOUND BOW STABILISATION

Being compact, nicely balanced and relatively heavy, a compound bow is usually easier to hold steady than a recurve. It is less sensitive to handle and string torque, and its limbs travel only a short distance between full draw and brace height. Characteristically, it is quick, smooth and not given to leaping around like a plain recurve bow. Consequently, it does not demand as much stabilisation. The majority of leading compound target and field archers rely on a long rod for stability, sometimes adding a counterweight on the inside of the handle for better balance and weight in-hand. A 30–36in rod with 1–4oz provides all the accuracy and forgiveness necessary to shoot perfect scores. For hunting, 6–10oz on a very short rod or attached directly to the handle offsets nervous twitches and slight shooting errors.

Perhaps because of their previous experience, many archers who switch from recurves to compounds insist on fitting heavy V-bars. Sometimes they get excellent results – though never better than a long rod can produce – but far more often they run into serious tuning and arrow matching problems because of excessive inertia and resistance around the arrow rest area. Instead of being launched cleanly, the arrow flicks against or in extreme cases ricochets off the bow. The answer is simple: take off the V-bar system.

TUNING

Experienced archers understand the need to retune the bow after the stabilisation is changed or adjusted. Normally this entails little more than a rerun of the bare shaft planing test or walk-back, followed by the appropriate alteration in button pressure,

A compound's V-bar unit should be light – if used at all.

centre shot and nocking height. Slightly increasing the weight, rod length or TFC pressure stiffens the arrow reaction by such a small amount that nothing needs be done. Indeed, a slightly stiff set-up often shoots better. Switching from a very light long rod – or no stabilisation at all – to a full V-bar arrangement, not only calls for drastic retuning but may well demand a different arrow specification as well. Sometimes a stiffer shaft is needed to clear the bow. Alternatively, a change of points or higher brace height might do the trick.

Archers with a full set-up who are unable to tune their bows may well benefit from taking off all but the long rod. Not only does the bow shoot more accurately (whether recurve or compound) but it also feels smoother and more controllable. This is also an excellent way to detect and correct errors of technique normally hidden by the more sophisticated arrangement. Indeed, some leading archers say that all changes of technique should be made with a lightly stabilised or even bare bow to highlight the drawbacks as well as the improvements.

5 Rests, Buttons and Clickers

RESTS

An arrow rest is much more than a means of holding the arrow against the bow while it is drawn and released. It must be precisely aligned with the bow's handle and limbs so that the arrow receives maximum energy and minimum radial deflection. While hard enough to encourage clean arrow launch, it must also yield to the occasional flick from shaft or vane. In theory, the arrow rest, handle pressure point and the centre of the bow should coincide. As this is obviously impossible, the grip pivot point is normally situated below bow centre while the pressure button sits above it, making an overall spacing of about two inches in most cases. The perfect dimension for any given bow is determined by laboratory and field tests, and the handle is subsequently bushed for a pressure button at that point.

Most manufacturers, including Yamaha, insist that arrow rest height should not be altered. Hoyt seem to disagree: the Gold Medalist recurve and Pro Medalist compound have vertical arrow rest adjustment as well as normal centre shot tuning. Raising or lowering the pressure button is an alternative to correcting arrow flight by moving the string nocking point. The archer can also compensate for personal factors such as how the structure of his hand matches the angle and pivot point of the grip. Opposites though they are, both systems work extremely well.

Adjustable for height or not, the pressure button obviously determines the position of the arrow rest itself: it should be set so that the middle of the button is aligned with, or slightly above, the centre line of the arrow. Contact must be maintained when the arrow starts to move forward. Without some vertical leeway there is a chance that the shaft might skid off the top of the button and foul against the window. On the other hand, the arrow must be tuned to give some lift under acceleration. Slight downward pressure between shaft and rest as the shaft begins its paradox cycle is an essential prelude to perfect arrow flight. A very soft rest causes the arrow point to dip; if the platform is rigid, the arrow rebounds too high and its back ends or vanes might occasionally clip the rest or handle hard enough to be thrown off course. An arrow rest should therefore be just resilient enough in the vertical plane to give adequate lift, but be soft and forgiving horizontally – precisely the characteristics of the flip rest design now universally popular with hunters and target archers.

Flip Rests

A hunting rest must be durable enough to withstand the hazards of terrain and weather as well as the pressures exerted by hunting weight shafts and high draw weights. With target bows, the emphasis is on sheer tuneability and accuracy instead. Unless bow and arrows are badly mismatched, the exact type of rest chosen is unlikely to spell the difference between good and bad results. Even so, it pays to test a range of models: almost certainly one in particular will give greater smoothness, easier tuning, cleaner launch and tighter grouping.

Features to consider are arm length, hinge pressure and vertical resistance. If the bow is

Flip rests respond well to the demands of high-performance tournament recurves.

cut well over-centre, or the arrow sits far from the window for some other reason, extra arm length is essential for security. Powerful target bows usually benefit from self-sprung wire arms as found on the Cavalier rest rather than the flimsier finger-type models. Sometimes choice is restricted by the shape of the bow handle: the under-arrow Flip II rest is too big for many slim handled bows like the Portland 2000. It is also important to check that the button protrudes far enough through the arrow rest body to operate properly. Where button travel is limited, a Hoyt Super Pro rest with the pressure plate cut off is a better choice.

Fixed Rests

The Hoyt Super Pro is one of the few remaining high quality rests designed to be shot with or without a pressure button. The arrow pushes on a spur of plastic designed to give adequate sideways support yet still be forgiving and easy to tune. Coupled to an adjustable centre shot plate, rests of this type are capable of extremely accurate shooting if the arrow is basically well matched to the bow, but are nowhere near as versatile as a pressure button and flip rest.

Cheaper fixed rests use a cushion of soft plastic, rubber or felt between arrow and bow handle. Useful for beginners' bows, these cheaper rests are completely the wrong

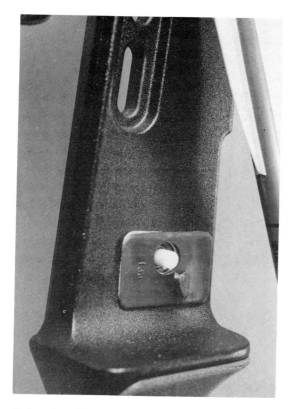

In hunting, the emphasis is as much on durability as on accuracy. A tough, simple fixed rest is usually the best choice.

choice for serious target shooting. In the hunting world, though, many excellent archers are quite happy to shoot from a heavy duty fixed rest. Simplicity and lack of mechanical parts are considered definite advantages in adverse conditions.

Compound Bow Rests

Most developments in the modern archery world are based on the compound bow, which is not only an exciting technical challenge in itself but also makes sense commercially as well, as compounds already take 90 per cent of the worldwide market. As yet, the engineering and design of the bow itself has not filtered through to accessories like arrow rests. Without doubt, they too will soon reflect modern technology – overdraws and inertia rests like the Barner are forerunners of sophisticated products to come.

At the moment, the compound world is dominated by two arrow rests: the pressure button/flip rest combination; and the spring rest, which is nothing more than a coil spring with one end straightened to support the arrow. The button system is ideal for hunting and finger release, while the spring rest generally gives better results for target shooting with a release aid. Finger release always produces a stronger paradox cycle and heavier arrow rest pressures than a release aid, so a pressure button offers more control and greater versatility than a plain spring, not only simplifying the tuning process but also giving greater insurance against mistakes. As with tournament recurves, there really is no better way to set up the bow for consistent, pin-point accuracy with a fair degree of forgiveness. Furthermore, hunters find the button and flip rest (or suitable fixed arm rest) more durable in the field and less sensitive when cold fingers increase string drag.

Given that bow and arrow are well matched, and nocking point and tiller settings are correct, the rest on a target compound shot with a release aid needs do little except support the front of the shaft in precise alignment with the string path. Release shooting creates such low paradox and arrow rest pressure that only a slight sideways cushioning is necessary. The only essential adjustment is in and out from the bow window to control centre shot alignment. A simple spring rest does the job perfectly with minimal need for tuning. There is no better way to extract maximum accuracy. Unfortunately though, it gives little compensation for mismatch between shaft and bow specifications. Changing springs gives limited

Flip rest and button (left) are considered ideal for hunting and finger shooting, whereas the spring rest gives enhanced target performance with a release.

scope because the different pressures available are basically intended to be used in step with bow draw weight. They do allow some flexibility in tuning, but not nearly as much as a pressure button. If the bow and arrow are nicely compatible, though, only centre shot adjustment should be necessary for perfect arrow flight.

The spring rest is also comparatively weak and gives only limited support for the arrow during draw and hold. Many finger shooters cannot use it even on a warm, still day. Imagine trying to balance a hunting shaft on a whisker of wobbling steel when the wind is blowing and your fingers are numb with cold. Problems escalate further with heavy,

large diameter shafts which are not only difficult to balance on the spring but also overwhelm it during release, especially if a cam bow is used. Taking all those factors into account, it is no wonder that serious hunters prefer to use a conventional button and rest even when shooting a release aid.

PRESSURE BUTTONS

The pressure button reduces paradox by absorbing some of the arrow's sideways bounce against the bow and gives some forgiveness of bad release. Of all the bow accessories ever invented, it is unquestionably the most valuable contribution to tuning and improved accuracy. Unfortunately, there is also a serious risk of destroying an inexperienced archer's performance and confidence, for the pressure button is by no means foolproof and can upset bow tuning so badly that not one arrow leaves the bow cleanly and the group is twice as big as it could be.

Pressure button quality varies enormously, but surprisingly there is little variation in performance. Expensive units precision-engineered from low friction metals and plastics are smoother and longer lasting than some of the cheap buttons, but for sheer tuneability the original brass Berger button controls an arrow equally well. Key design points are smooth spring action and a reasonably sturdy pressure pad, resistant to grooving and wide enough to support the arrow properly when it flies past.

In almost every case where an archer finds it impossible to use a button, spring pressure and centre shot alignment are wrong. Some coaches and dealers still insist that 8oz of pressure is enough and that the arrow should be set exactly on bow centre. Very few archers, including many of world class standard, are able to tune properly and shoot consistently on that basis. Even on low draw weight bows, spring pressure should be in excess of 12oz. On the average high performance target recurve in the 40–45lb bracket, somewhere around 20oz is recommended as a starting point for experiment. As for centre shot alignment, the overwhelming consensus is that the arrow should be set well left of the centre line (for a right-handed archer).

Pressure and alignment are interrelated. As a rough working principle for gaining experience with pressure button tuning, the lower the tension, the further out from the window the arrow must be, and vice versa. Some archers tune by presetting the centre shot (normally about an arrow's width left of

Big differences in price and smoothness are seldom reflected in the results. A cheap brass button gives satisfactory tuning.

centre, as shown in the Easton selection matrix booklet) then altering spring pressure. This works very well. However, increasing numbers of target archers find that presetting the button to moderate tension, say 12–16oz, then adjusting centre shot to produce clean launch and minimum cycling gives even better results with much less effort. When that basic setting is established, exact tuning is completed using the walkback technique which is self-diagnostic of button pressure and centre-shot alignment. Some experts say that although the walkback pattern is extremely accurate, it does not necessarily guarantee the tightest groups and almost certainly does not give maximum

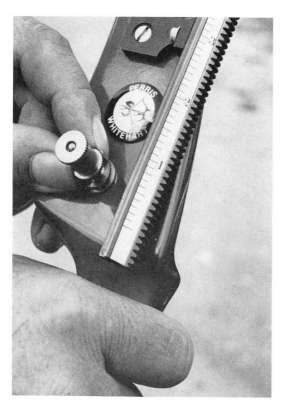

Spring tension and centre shot are interrelated, so the button must have a wide enough range of adjustment to handle the many possible combinations.

forgiveness. A better method is to work through the various combinations of centre shot and pressure to discover which offers the best balance of grouping power, sight setting and compensation for error.

Taking into consideration the three options of light, medium and high spring tension with their corresponding centre shot settings, most archers find that the medium generally gives the best all round performance. Whatever specific bare shaft impact point or walk-back pattern this produces should be taken as the reference point for future work; for example, the bare shaft hits slightly low and left of the fletched group, or the arrow pattern between 10 and 35 metres

shows a curved bias towards the left at the middle distances. This personal deviation from the usually recommended results can only be discovered by careful trial and error. Ultimately, of course, on-target grouping and ease of shooting are much more important than any tuning exercise and should always be the final test.

CLICKERS

How important is the clicker in recurve target archery? Upwards of middle rank tournament work – beyond 1000 FITA, for the sake of argument – the clicker is a great help in achieving high, consistent scores. At the very top of the tree, it is considered absolutely essential for maximum accuracy. There is, however, one equally powerful argument for not using a clicker: it is a major reason for the failure of a novice or inexperienced archer to develop proper technique and control.

Clicker theory is simple enough: draw the arrow almost through the blade, aim, pull through to produce the click, and let go. Anyone can see that by watching a top class archer put arrow after arrow in the gold. Almost all problems result from the mistaken idea that the clicker controls the shot. If it does, the clicker inevitably controls the archer as well. A direct result of this is that the majority of archers not only struggle with the clicker, but cannot shoot at all without one; they are completely at the mercy of that strip of spring steel.

Clicker Technique

Clicker technique is effortless and accurate only when the archer himself controls the shooting process from preparation to follow-through. As the draw builds up, the arrow's position under the clicker *confirms* to the expert archer that:

1. He is establishing the correct foundation for the shot.
2. The arrow is drawn the correct distance.

It is essential to understand the difference between this approach and the haphazard, uncontrolled draw used by so many unsuccessful archers. All they think about is reaching full draw in some fashion, then hauling the point through the clicker. The resultant set-up at full draw looks the same in each case, but alignment and forces of body, bow and arrow are very different indeed. As the draw has such enormous bearing on release, follow-through and accuracy, the potential advantages of the clicker are already lost.

The expert does not struggle to make the device click. In modern archery, string release is increasingly regarded as nothing more than a transitional stage between hold and follow-through. Release *and the click that triggers it* are simply one more step in the archer's style and rhythm. He could – 90 per cent of the time anyway – shoot perfectly well without it. Of course, the click does help to smooth out the release and ideally will make it a totally subconscious reaction; this is precisely why a clicker is such a valuable

Clicker control 1 *Stance and body angle help determine clicker position.*

factor in championship archery. But the important, though subtle, distinction remains: the clicker enhances the archer's control and boosts his confidence by confirming what he already knows and freeing his mind to concentrate on more important areas. Archers who struggle, focus their minds so strongly on the physical aspects of the release that their form loses fluidity or even freezes a fraction of an inch before the blade drops.

Clicker Set-up

A clicker should not be introduced until the archer has learned to shoot fairly well. For one thing, it is usually better to superimpose the clicker on an already established style than to develop style around the clicker itself. Also, a clicker cannot be fitted correctly until the archer's form and draw length are firmly developed – and draw length usually increases by at least half an inch during the first year.

Once those foundations are established there should be no difficulty involved in setting up the device. The blade should be adjusted so that no more than $\frac{1}{4}$in of point lies under it when the archer is at full draw and on aim. The exact overhang is controlled by watching the arrow itself during the draw, or by using a two-stage clicker which operates on a similar principle to that of taking up first

Clicker control 2 *Draw with the back muscles to achieve good tension and alignment.*

pressure on a rifle trigger.

Although draw length itself should never be compromised, arrow length and hence clicker position can be varied, sometimes with great benefit. Classically, the arrow point should lie about half an inch forward of the pressure button. If there is no chance of draw length being increased, and tuning is perfect, there is no reason to stray from that. If the archer feels that he might want to pull a little further in the foreseeable future – say he intends to try a side of face anchor – it makes more sense to choose arrows that extend about an inch past the button. Setting the clicker position accordingly gives half an inch leeway for future experiment.

Varying the arrow length sometimes assists with tuning. If a 2014 arrow of the 'correct' length is a shade too whippy but a 2114 of the same length is too stiff, there is usually enough room on modern bows to shift the clicker further forward and thereby gain an inch or more on arrow length. Now the bigger shaft tunes perfectly. If the clicker lies at such a shallow angle that the end of the blade tends to flick the point off the arrow rest, it should be remounted vertically on an extension block glued or screwed to the bow handle. Check to see if the arrow 'hops' from under the blade by drawing through the clicker without releasing; it is very difficult to detect this while actually shooting. The

Clicker control 3 *No more than ¼in of arrow should remain under the clicker at full draw.*

Clicker control 4 *Release should be automatic, leading straight into follow-through.*

result of an unstable point is bad grouping and erratic arrow flight, both of which are much more likely to be blamed on tuning or shooting error. The real cause sometimes goes undetected for months.

6 Arrow Dynamics

An arrow's accuracy, kinetic energy (striking power), penetration and in-flight stability depend upon the transfer of energy from the archer and his bow to the shaft during and immediately after the release. These factors seem obvious when written, but in everyday shooting on range and in the field they are often ignored. Perfect arrows shot from a modest quality bow fly more accurately and strike more effectively than bad shafts shot by the world's finest bow. At the highest levels of target shooting and hunting, regardless of the kind of bow used – compound, recurve or even ancient longbow – successful archers have always insisted on the best arrows available and they always will.

Nothing in the way of tuning and tackle can transform an inept shooter into a champion, but there is every reason to believe that technique itself and the inner confidence that supports it are highly dependent on equipment response. A well set-up bow shooting nicely matched arrows is not only capable of shooting excellent scores but also responds predictably to mistakes. The deviation pattern of the wayward shafts is therefore diagnostic as well, which it cannot be if the bow is badly set-up.

In such a situation, the archer can see exactly how control and technique are developing and detect specific areas of weakness. Such positive feedback puts the emphasis where it should be – on the archer himself. He therefore works harder, shoots better and gains more confidence, which underpins his technique, produces even better results and gives yet more encouragement to work harder still; a highly desirable cycle of cause and effect.

Without the right arrow in his bow, no archer can be sure that the groups properly reflect his efforts. It is quite common for an archer to shoot for years with a good bow and sound style yet fail to realise his full potential, achieving low tournament placings, and as a hunter seldom making a clean kill and sometimes missing for no apparent reason. If he does not care about the quality and specification of his arrows, an archer is gambling

Compared to firearms, even the fastest compound bow is hopelessly slow. Don't expect miracles from arrow speed or trajectory.

with every shot he makes.

Arrows badly matched to bow or archer *and* inconsistent one to another are even more destructive of technique, score and confidence. Six perfectly set-up, aimed and executed shots with the wrong arrows might easily result in an 18in group at 30 yards. Exactly the same shots made with well matched, properly maintained arrows could go into a 4in circle or smaller. Thousands of target shooters and hunters are not only unaware of the situation, but spend huge sums of money on equipment and years of effort and frustration trying to correct it by the 'logical' process of buying better bows, working on technique and practising for hours on end. Compared to all that, the cost of good arrows immediately becomes an investment rather than an unnecessary expense. Because modern bows are so highly tuneable, one might even conclude that it is better to buy a bow to suit the arrows instead of vice versa. Some expert archers actually do that. The only snag is that first you must determine exactly which shaft you need.

Knowledge and careful calculation help narrow the field to a shortlist of potentially suitable arrows, but only shooting them can determine exactly which is best. Even then the question arises: best for what? A perfect arrow for indoors might not be ideal for outdoor FITA; a broadhead hunting shaft might not be so accurate and predictable when armed with a field point for practice shooting or bowhunter events; a bow shot with a release aid might require other shafts for finger shooting.

SPEED, WEIGHT AND STABILITY

Any bow's performance is inevitably limited by its energy source, the archer's muscles. Consequently, the kinetic energy and speed of an arrow (its muzzle velocity and muzzle energy, so to speak) are minimal compared to those of firearms. Regardless of modern compound designs and advanced engineering materials, the fastest and most efficient of bows is still a low powered weapon whose limitations highlight the need for a realistic attitude. Faster, harder hitting, flatter-shooting – such claims convey the impression that some bows are considerably more accurate and lethal than others. In fact, improvements are usually not only small but almost inevitably pay a penalty in stability and accuracy. Overemphasising any aspect of arrow performance produces a deficiency or backlash elsewhere.

Arrow Velocity

Within reason, a bow shoots a light arrow faster than a heavy one. Heavy and light in this case mean the upper and lower limits of the range of shafts recommended by the Easton matrix for the bow in question. Many experienced archers would also include shafts in the next higher poundage band as well, on the basis that most bows shoot better with the extra stiffness and weight.

Judging overall bow performance by velocity figures alone, many archers automatically choose the lightest shafts available for their poundage and length: target archers assume that a fast arrow is more accurate because it flies flatter and is exposed to the wind for a shorter period; hunters equate high velocity with greater penetration. While the concept of high velocity has merit, in practice it is often self-defeating.

Advantages of high speed are:

1. Flatter trajectory.
2. Less time for wind to divert the arrow.
3. Arrow clears the bow more rapidly.

Its disadvantages are:

1. Lower bow efficiency.
2. Inherently less stable during release.
3. Usually, lower momentum.
4. Increased air drag.
5. More critical of technique.
6. More difficult to tune.
7. Less consistent performance.

Bow Efficiency

The efficiency of a bow expressed as a percentage of its stored energy is lower with light arrows because limbs and string cannot transfer all that energy into the arrow nock, and the shaft itself is unable to make best use of what it does receive. Light arrows usually fly more rapidly than heavy ones but the gain is less than theory suggests. In some cases speed may actually drop if the arrow is so light that it and the bow are highly unstable during release. Switching to a heavier shaft not only produces greater smoothness, quietness and forgiveness but may also produce equal or even higher velocity.

Some archers consider that a light, rapidly accelerating arrow encourages a clean, consistent release. The arrow clears the bow very quickly, so it is also less likely to be affected by minor errors in shooting technique. That is the theory, anyway. A com-

Velocity tests reveal interesting results. For example, a heavier arrow might be faster.

pound bow shot with a release aid bears this out provided that tuning and technique are of very high standards, but in everyday hunting and tournament work there are severe penalities. Recurves and high-performance cam bows could well prove impossible to control with finger release.

By shooting heavier and preferably stiffer arrows, most archers see immediate improvements in grouping and tuneability. A bow that reacted nervously and viciously to light arrows becomes smooth, friendly and inspires confidence. Unfortunately, the new arrow will probably fly more slowly than before, and if there is one aspect of archery guaranteed to upset the apple cart, losing velocity is it. For many target shooters and hunters it is an unforgivable sin. But is it so unforgivable? Let us consider exactly what the penalties of losing velocity are.

Trajectory

Flight path flatness and sight settings are important considerations in accurate shooting. In general, a slow arrow has a more pronounced trajectory. Long distance settings will be lower on the sight track, and range estimation calls for greater skills and accuracy. Taken at face value, these are major disadvantages although in practice they usually resolve themselves easily enough. Today's bows are remarkably efficient weapons, more than capable of providing a comfortable sight setting for the longest FITA distances of 90 metres for men and 70 metres for women. Even light, well-tuned bows drawing about 38lb and 32lb respectively shoot reasonably flat at those distances. FITA and most other target events are shot over set distances, so in many ways an arrow's flight parabola is of no consequence. Once calibrated, sight settings should remain consistent from one tournament to

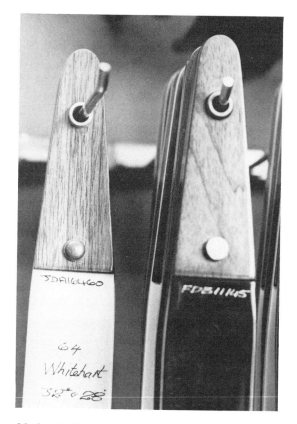

Modern limbs are so good that 90m and 70m sight marks should never be difficult to achieve even at moderate poundage.

the next unless equipment set-up and technique are altered.

It could be argued that a fast flying arrow needs less adjustment to sight elevation to allow for wind, but in reality this is another idea that owes more to theory than to actual shooting. Some target archers who change to heavier arrows discover that long range settings are actually improved because the bow works more efficiently, the arrow is launched more cleanly and, due to its extra weight, the shaft has greater 'carry' in flight (more scientifically, lower drag and higher momentum).

Hunters and field shooters who must estimate range would obviously benefit from a very flat arrow path. However, since it is universally agreed that hunters should make it a priority to get close to their quarry, perhaps this is less important than suggested by manufacturers of ever-faster bows that rely on light arrows for their speed. All arrows not only drop, but drop quickly. In comparison with firearms, the best arrows are pitifully inadequate. When we say that an arrow shoots flat, we really mean it shoots with less drop than some of the others; it certainly does not maintain the same sight mark from fifteen yards to fifty, nor even between ten and twenty.

The implication is that a fast arrow reduces the need to estimate distances or to aim so accurately. However, a few shots with even the flattest flying arrows show that over the everyday hunting ranges of 15–35 yards, drop is considerable – better than on old, slower equipment perhaps, but significant all the same. The archer still carries a heavy responsibility to shoot within his limitations, although practice at range estimation plus a properly calibrated multi-pin sight will certainly help minimise errors. Bearing in mind that heavy arrows are an important factor in successful hunting and clean kills, perhaps hunters should think deeply before committing themselves to a fast, light arrow.

Shooting at unmarked distances over 50

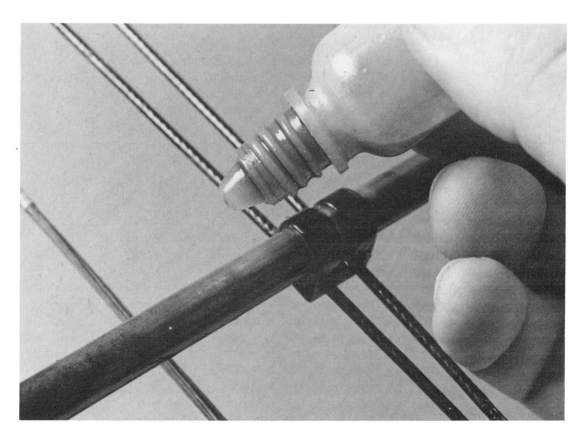

Cable guard and wheel axle drag reduce both shot-to-shot consistency and velocity. Peak performance calls for regular, careful maintenance.

yards, field archers are most affected by arrow trajectory characteristics. A five-yard error in estimation at the longer ranges can easily produce a complete miss. A particularly hard-shooting bow would certainly prove invaluable. On the other hand scores approached maximum long before the introduction of compound bows, never mind overdraws and energy cams. How often is lack of speed an excuse for lack of expertise rather than a valid reason for missing?

Roughly speaking, to drop half as far at any given range an arrow must fly twice as fast. For the moment at least, velocity increases of this order are technically impossible. Cam bow enthusiasts who like to give the impression that their bows shoot almost as flat as a hunting rifle are fooling nobody but themselves. The only way a bow can shoot as flat as a rifle is for the arrow to fly as fast as a bullet. Considering that 250 feet per second is exceptionally quick for an arrow while 2500 feet per second is pretty slow for a medium calibre bullet, archery still has a long way to go.

Drift and Drag

The laws of air drag and drift show there are no easy solutions to how far and how predictably an arrow will be affected by wind and turbulence. Some archers maintain that a light, fast arrow drifts less because it is exposed to the elements for only a short while; others say that a heavier but slower flying shaft calls for greater allowances, but then holds its course better due to the higher momentum and lower drag.

Of the factors involved in creating air drag, the most important is velocity. Given the choice between a light, fast arrow and a slow, heavier shaft shot from the same bow, the latter should be less vulnerable to wind and air turbulence, or at least more predict-

able in its arc of drift. Physics aside, there are other reasons why a heavier arrow generally gives better results in adverse conditions. Probably the major cause of inaccurate shooting in the wind lies inside the archer's head. Unable to maintain a perfect sight picture because the pin drifts erratically across the target, he becomes tense. Tension destroys the smooth execution of the shot, so the group not only opens up considerably but the arrows themselves come out of the bow flirting, 'porpoising' and less stable than normal. Unaware of the real cause of his problems, he blames the wind for spraying his shots all over the target.

Rather than strive for perfect aiming, concentrate on making relaxed, controlled shots. An archer who persists in fighting the wind is amazed how well his groups hold up when the mental approach changes. Excellent target archers say that up to a certain point wind has little or no effect on group size. Scores are lower because the occasional arrow deviates due to a sudden gust or because the bow arm is blown out of alignment as the arrow is released. Only when conditions are severe, with no pattern to wind direction and strength, is the group itself destroyed.

Assuming that the archer maintains his form, arrow drift may not prove too troublesome regardless of arrow weight and speed. A great deal depends on tuning. If a well-tuned shaft leaves a bow cleanly, the vanes do not need to work too hard, nor must they be large to provide the necessary spin and steerage. Characteristically, the arrow will fly straight for 20–50 yards before assuming a slightly head-to-wind angle, then drift smoothly to the target. Having a higher momentum, a heavy arrow is more likely to hold this flight pattern. A lighter arrow is more vulnerable because it lacks 'carry', and also generates more air resistance because of

Overemphasis on aiming in the wind causes tension, which aggravates the effects of natural drift and scatter.

its higher speed (assuming a similar shaft length and surface area). Already it is more at risk.

The Speed Penalty

A very fast, light arrow is inevitably more difficult to tune and less forgiving of technique than a heavier shaft shot from the same bow. Often it needs bigger vanes for stability, which create disproportionately high air drag. Lower in momentum as well, it lacks the sheer guts to maintain a steady flight path at long range and is always more sensitive to gusts and eddies. Worse than all that, it reacts violently to the slightest deviation in shooting form, generally the first thing to break down in bad weather.

The arrow's centre of gravity can affect accuracy depending upon shaft length and diameter, weight, wall thickness and shooting style. Balance point is more critical with light, fast arrows; aluminium/carbon shafts are particularly difficult to handle in this respect, demanding immaculate technique and perfect tuning even in still air. Like standard aluminium shafts, these specialist arrows can be individually balanced with high density inserts, though it is doubtful whether the process offers significant advantages for all but a few world class archers. Indeed, many of these people question the value of 'high-tech' shafts anyway. Over the years a slowish, stiff shaft has become the

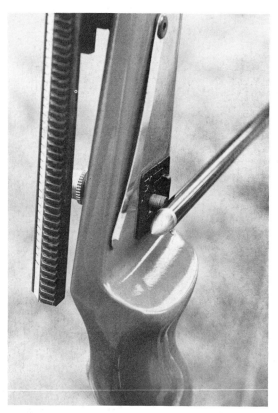

Point weight controls the arrow's centre of gravity and therefore its stability and drift pattern as well.

Penetration

Arrow penetration is a controversial subject: which is the more important, speed or arrow weight? Assuming that the arrow leaves the bow cleanly, excellent point design and high momentum are probably the most decisive factors. Laboratory penetration tests and practical hunting observations bear out the idea very well. Preoccupation with arrow speed can be as counter-productive in hunting as it is in target shooting. The trend towards light, short arrows, high weight cam bows and overdraw devices often results in an outfit that is inherently unstable and difficult to shoot. At the same time, the increase in arrow performance over that of a more stable and conventional outfit is marginal. Since momentum is probably more useful than feet per second in promoting maximum penetration, the quest for speed is self-defeating in that respect as well, which explains why many authorities on hunting are adamant that some of the latest trends spell nothing but trouble.

They recommend a full length, fairly heavy arrow shot from a well-tuned conventional compound or recurve. Coupled with high quality broadheads and reasonably good technique, these ensure the reliable, humane kills which should be the hunter's primary goal. As for broadheads themselves, while some show up better in laboratory tests and each has its devotees, every one of the popular models is more than capable of holding its own on soft skinned game taken at realistic distances. An arrow kills by cutting not by impact shock as firearms do, therefore a hunter's priority is to deliver his shot with pin-point accuracy under the most rigorous field conditions. A well-placed arrow from a bow in the 50–70lb class is more than sufficient to kill cleanly and quickly; most men can handle a compound of that weight with

classic choice for top level recurve shooting.

Compound bows are capable of handling lighter, more flexible arrows than could be shot cleanly from a recurve of equivalent poundage. A release aid offers even more scope to use very light shafts due to the low paradox reaction when the string accelerates. The third and latest factor is the overdraw device which effectively raises velocity by allowing the archer to draw a short arrow inside the bow handle. In all, a properly tuned and shot compound bow is capable of producing high arrow speeds and reasonable control. Unfortunately, the system positively encourages the archer to strive for arrow speed pure and simple. Inevitably there is a risk of overdoing it.

The old longbow is traditional proof that momentum is extremely important for good penetration. The heavy but relatively slow arrow has enormous driving power.

relative ease when their muscles are conditioned.

By contrast, the archer struggling to pull and aim too heavy a weapon, or fighting to control an ultra-fast, 'nervous' outfit, is far more likely to miss or wound. Besides, a badly handled weapon often gives lower energy figures than a well-shot bow of considerably lower draw weight. Because most archers underestimate a bow and arrow's lethal force anyway, much lighter bows than those in the popular weight range could be used with confidence for the vast majority of hunting. A 30lb recurve shooting razor-sharp broadheads would probably do the trick. However, legislation controlling minimum bow and arrow specifications is a sensible measure. Without it, a few determined souls would inevitably compete to see who could kill the biggest animal with the lightest bow – an exact parallel with line-class fishing records.

Target Penetration

Tournament archers are only concerned with having enough arrow penetration to prevent regular bounce-outs from the target. Otherwise it is more practical not to drive arrows deep into the boss where they are difficult to withdraw and in extreme circumstances may bend or distort. High-density compressed straw targets pose a special threat to badly tuned, thin walled arrows shot indoors, occasionally snapping a shaft which enters the target face at an oblique angle. Data collected from the tournament world suggests that fast, light arrows are more prone to excessive bounce-out, and that some target materials are more nuisance than others. Surprisingly, a soft, springy target centre is often much worse than a really hard face. This is entirely consistent with arrow dynamics in general and underlines the enormous value of using reasonably heavy shafts instead of tuning the outfit for pure speed.

7 Arrow Shafts

SELECTION CHARTS

Selection tables and charts are a great help in narrowing down the choice of an arrow, but they are far from complete. Some are based on outdated bow designs, and few take into account the huge differences between archers themselves. Recommendations also go wrong when arrows are fitted with non-standard points. Add other variables due to vane drag, shooting style, tuning skill, stabiliser preferences, string weight and material,

and it's no wonder that confusion arises. Easton's selection matrix, which compares shaft diameter, wall thickness and alloy specification to draw weight and shaft length, is by far the best chart but still needs a certain amount of personal interpretation. As Easton themselves advise, shaft recommendations are never definitive. The figures are based on basic stiffness/weight combinations that generally prove suitable for hunting and target work, but they certainly do not guarantee a perfect match to the bow.

Every bow and arrow responds specifically to the individual archer.

If you shoot a 28in arrow from a 40lb recurve target bow, the chart recommends half a dozen shafts ranging from 1913 to 1818. But precisely which one will be best for you? No formula can be applied with absolute success, though it would probably be better to choose one of the 0.014–0.016in walled shafts for target work because they offer an ideal combination of strength and performance. Thinner walls tend to be rather fragile, and thick walled arrows sometimes feel dull and unresponsive. Hunting shaft selection follows much the same pattern, with an obviously desirable bias towards durability.

All charts are based on that mythical being the 'average' archer. No two people shoot in exactly the same way, consequently any specified bow and arrow will react differently according to who tunes and shoots it. Handle torque and pressure point, string grip, release, back tension and even body weight are a few of the variables to be considered. As a result, bow efficiency and accuracy vary considerably from one archer to the next. The following shows the arrow speed obtained by six archers shooting 28in, 1816 X7s from a 38lb target recurve individually tuned by each archer before he used the chronograph.

Archer	Average Arrow Speed
A	165 f.p.s.
B	186 f.p.s.
C	194 f.p.s.
D	159 f.p.s.
E	191 f.p.s.
F	171 f.p.s.

The 38 f.p.s. spread alone suggests that an 1816 is not the perfect choice for everyone: the slowest archer achieved very poor sight settings at 90 metres and would benefit from either a few more pounds of draw weight, if he could handle them, or a lighter shaft. More significantly, Archer E found it impossible to tune the outfit even though velocity was close to that of Archer C whose arrows shot beautifully. Judged by the relative impact point of a bare tuning shaft, 1816s were much too whippy for him. 1914s gave a considerable improvement with hardly any change in velocity, and 1916s, though obviously stiff, still grouped tightly at 90 metres with a comfortable sight setting.

Although the only way to find the perfect arrow is by experiment, the basic recommendations do allow the majority of archers to pick a first set of arrows that perform well enough to give acceptable results. But it is

Centre shot must be adjusted to suit the arrow's paradox reaction.

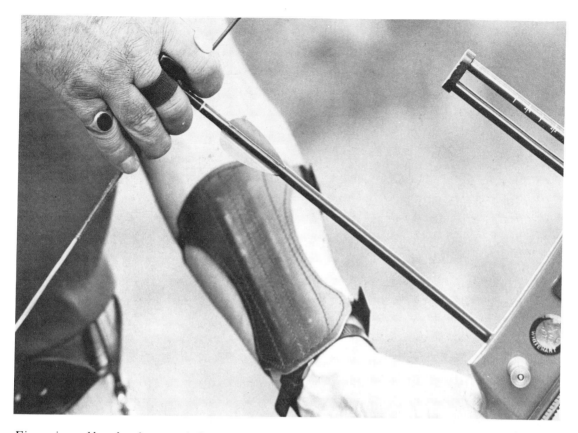

Finger size and bow hand pressure influence the shaft's reaction. An arrow which matches one archer might be wrong for another who shoots the same length and poundage.

worth bearing in mind that the range of diameters and walls suggested are not merely alternatives to each other; nor is an X7 always interchangeable with an XX75 or other alloy of the same wall and diameter. Harmonic response due to the crystalline structure of the aluminium alloy may seem to be an obscure characteristic of an arrow, but can sometimes produce a noticeable effect on grouping power.

RECURVE CHARACTERISTICS

Modern tournament recurve bows, heavily stabilised and Kevlar strung, often react more predictably and shoot tighter groups if the arrow is stiffer and/or heavier than recommended. Some bows are more demanding because their stored energy values, draw force pattern and limb recovery speed are substantially above average. Just as six archers pulling the one bow produce widely varying arrow velocities, so bows of the same draw weight but different in make, length and limb materials show markedly different performance figures.

Changing from a 40lb bow of old design to a modern tournament weapon, you may not be able to shoot the same arrows as before because the new bow overpowers them. There are no hard and fast rules, but in general with today's high performance bows it pays to test shafts in the next stiffness band up of the Easton matrix. Switching from a regular 1914 to a theoretically over-stiff 2014 may work wonders: although the softer shaft performs quite well, the 2014 may prove easier to tune, group more tightly and add forgiveness.

COMPOUND CHARACTERISTICS

The compound bow's speed is mainly due to its ability to handle lighter arrows than could be shot by a recurve of the same draw weight. The string accelerates the arrow quite gently over the first few inches after release then steps up to full power. The arrow is more stable and far less affected by paradox oscillations. Shot with a release aid which further reduces paradox, a well-tuned compound bow should easily handle arrows impossibly light and whippy for the equivalent weight recurve. The manufacturers' recommendation of averaging peak and let-off weights as the basis for arrow selection is an excellent starting point for buying target and hunting shafts, but most of the limitations and provisos of recurve arrow selection still apply. The lighter the arrow, the more unforgiving and critical it will be – even shot with a release aid.

All things being equal, the lightest possible arrow capable of shooting cleanly from the bow will produce the highest velocity. But in target and hunting, things are rarely equal. Good tuning and a release aid cannot prevent a distinct 'nervousness' in the bow as

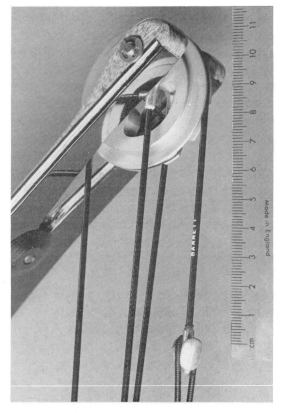

Factory specifications like cable pigtail length control the bow's performance. As such, they are a vital basis for shaft selection and tuning.

lighter and lighter arrows are shot. The over-draw device aggravates matters because a compound bow's in-built stability is determined by the triangle formed by the axles and handle pressure point. Drawing the arrow point inside that triangle inevitably makes the system more sensitive to shooting and tuning errors. In subjective terms, an overdrawn cam bow is about ten times harder to shoot accurately.

As with recurves, the only sensible course is to test a range of shafts to determine which offers a superior combination of accuracy, forgiveness and performance. Increasingly, archers are prepared to forgo a few feet per second to achieve those highly desirable features. Compound shafts are affected by variations in the archer's tuning and shooting skills. Surveys among bow hunters and target archers indicates that arrow speed and kinetic energy vary far more than on recurves. Some archers shooting 45lb peak weight bows produce higher stored and kinetic energy figures than those with 70lb. The obvious explanation is that a well-tuned outfit, shot with skill, is far more efficient than a much heavier but ill-tuned, badly shot bow. Even among bows of the same draw weight, arrow speeds and kinetic energy figures may differ by 50 per cent or more between individual archers. Cam bows seem especially vulnerable, though the pattern is noticeable with the lower performance wheel eccentrics as well.

The answer lies in better technique and tuning and, above all, in choosing relatively heavy, stiff shafts that allow the bow to perform with higher efficiency and stability. High-performance cam bows shot from the fingers may well benefit from an arrow close to that recommended for a recurve of the same peak weight. Calculations based on averaged peak/let-off weight are likely to produce unreliable results at best; sometimes the shaft is impossible to shoot cleanly.

High-performance cam bows are highly sensitive to shaft weight and stiffness. The matrix chart's recommendation may not apply.

RELEASE TECHNIQUE

Complete relaxation of the finger muscles coupled with proper back tension certainly produce excellent consistency in release, but there are still limitations in the cleanliness of the string's escape due to the size and weight of the fingers themselves. In accordance with the law that action and reaction are equal and opposite, despite an absolutely inert release where the string really does produce the desired pushing aside of the fingers, its path will still be deflected to some degree. Variation between archers' fingers explains why some people can shoot fairly low spined arrows whereas others whose technique seems equally good cannot achieve proper bow clearance and grouping power at the same poundage without using much stiffer shafts.

If, despite good technique and proper bow set-up, you cannot prevent a bare tuning shaft of the recommended specification from impacting to the right of the fletched group (right-handed archer), perhaps that is the reason. A stiffer and, perhaps, heavier arrow might do the trick. Sometimes the pattern is reversed: the recommended shaft hits left

Nocking point height and security are vitally important to a clean release.

regardless of tuning, in other words it reacts stiffly. This may be due to particularly small, light fingers that hardly disturb the string's path. Within reason, though, slightly stiff shafts usually group well and are extra-forgiving, so no changes are necessary.

KINETIC ENERGY CALCULATION

It is generally accepted that an arrow's kinetic energy (KE) reflects comparative bow performance and, all things being equal, the arrow's potential for trajectory, range and, arguably, accuracy and penetration. It is unlikely that anybody has won a target championship or put meat on the table by knowing the KE of his arrows, but the figures make useful and interesting data for the enthusiast.

Kinetic energy is the energy possessed by an object due to its motion, and is calculated from the formula: KE equals half the mass multiplied by the square of velocity. The unit of measurement is the foot-pound (ft/lb). To save complicated conversions from grains to pounds and allowing for acceleration due to gravity and other technical details, a practical formula for archers is:

$$KE = \frac{\text{weight of arrow in grains} \times \text{velocity in feet per second}}{450,240}$$

The total weight of the arrow – shaft, point, nock and vanes – is what counts. Arrow velocity is to be measured at an appropriate distance from the bow by a chronograph. Generally, KE figures are based on the 'muzzle velocity' about three feet from the handle. More meaningful figures for penetration might be calculated by taking velocity readings just in front of the target instead.

Velocity changes due to bow tuning, shaft specification, technique and stabilisation show up on the chronograph and influence the result. Thus, a series of experiments should reveal the characteristics of both archer and his equipment. Within reason, KE figures can be directly compared to each other since, all things being equal (how often that applies to bow and arrow performance), high KE is a sign of proper set-up, tuning and style. What you cannot do is use the formula to predict the velocity of an untested shaft, because bow efficiency changes in step with arrow weight and often with stiffness as well.

The lighter the arrow the less efficient the bow becomes; increases in arrow speed and KE are nowhere near those predicted by mathematics. Raising arrow weight usually

Chronograph readings are the basis of KE calculation.

increases the bow's efficiency and therefore boosts KE beyond the expected figure. On much the same theme, heavy draw weight bows are often less efficient than bows in the average 40–65lb target and hunting categories. Even with the appropriate arrows a .75lb compound rarely achieves a 50 per cent KE advantage over a 50lb bow. A glaring characteristic of many heavy bows is that the archer works extremely hard to gain virtually nothing.

SHAFT MATERIALS

Except at the very lowest levels of school and recreational archery, aluminium alloy arrows dominate the sport. Of the arrows shot in club, national and international events, Eastons reign supreme. A similar pattern emerges from the hunting world, with more than 90 per cent of archers using Easton aluminium. In some respects, excellent arrow shafts of graphite and other materials are unfairly overlooked. Modern reinforced plastic shafts are tough, straight, accurate and reliable, probably at least the equal of aluminium for hunting. In some key areas like durability, impact absorption and diameter/stiffness ratios, advanced fibres like graphite, boron and even Kevlar are potentially superior.

As only a small number of archers use advanced fibres regularly, it is extremely difficult to collect enough practical information to allow fair comparisons, although range and field tests suggest that any high-grade hunting product in this category – Graphlex being the classic example – is more than capable of holding its own. As target shafts, advanced fibres are not in the same class as XX75 and X7 due to inferior performance, wider quality tolerances and a limited choice of weight and stiffness. Conventional target points are generally unavailable. Overall, there arises in archers' minds a doubt about taking a chance on anything other than Easton. It must be frustrating for the specialist arrow manufacturer; but perhaps a great deal could be gained by aggressive marketing. Much the same thinking applies to advanced aluminium/carbon and fluted aluminium shafts. So few archers shoot them just now that no meaningful data exists about what the ordinary archer could expect to gain, if anything.

Alloy Choice

The main question is whether to invest in X7, XX75 or the less expensive Easton 24 and Gamegetter shafts. Properly assembled and matched to the bow, carefully maintained and accurately shot, any of these shafts performs exceedingly well. Easton 24 and Gamegetters, being of fairly tough alloy, absorb a reasonable amount of punishment. Their straightness tolerances are less than

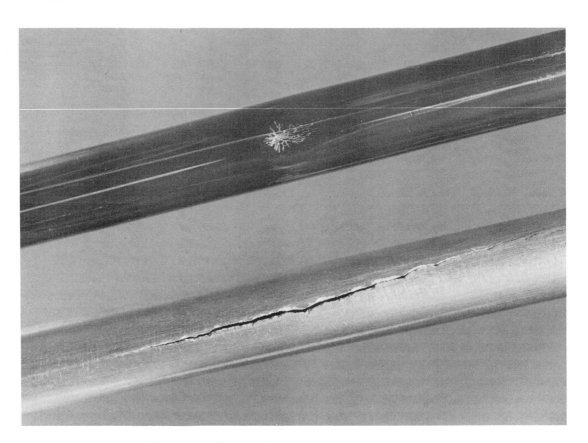

Above: impact damage. The arrow is still shootable.
Below: stress cracks in X7 alloy are dangerous.

those of higher grade shafts, but they are still capable of extremely good groups. Their main disadvantages are a medium life-span and some restriction in bow matching; light wall shafts are not available, for example.

XX75 shafts are substantially tougher, more resistant to bending and available in the light walled, stiff specifications of special interest to target archers. The gold XX75 target shaft is marginally superior in accuracy due to its improved straightness tolerance compared to the hunting versions, but in reality this amounts to little or nothing. It is extremely doubtful whether anyone but the very best of tournament archers could differentiate between them on grouping power.

X7s are the premier target shaft of all time. With tolerances so low that for all practical purposes it can be considered absolutely straight and uniform, the X7 is also highly resistant to bending. No other arrow withstands such a beating from today's high performance bows yet continues to deliver superb accuracy with minimal need for maintenance. Its only disadvantage is actually linked to those outstanding qualities: damaged shafts tend to retain their bend or even split rather than straighten. An X7 deflected by a wooden target leg or even from the straw itself may snap immediately. Occasionally an undamaged shaft will self-destruct in its box, torn apart by internal stresses in the alloy crystals.

So which grade should an archer choose? Despite the excellent results achieved with Easton 24s, Eagles or Gamegetters – or indeed other cheap alloy shafts like Sherwood and Sonic – the cost of an XX75 or even an X7 is so small compared to every other aspect of archery that these high quality shafts are not only justified in performance terms and in greater choice of walls and diameters, but are often cheaper in the long run as well. A set of well-maintained target XX75s or X7s last at least five years. Service life of a hunting arrow is less important in some ways and losses are inevitable, but nobody can afford to compromise on quality when the trophy of a lifetime may be at stake on his next trip.

8   Fletching, Nocks and Points

FLETCHING

The priority in shaft selection and bow tuning is to create the best possible conditions for arrow launch: precise injection of bow energy into the nock, clean bow clearance plus minimal residual oscillation of the shaft during its first few yards of free flight. After that, the arrow's inherent stability due to length, weight and balance point should take over. Under these desirable conditions the fletching system enhances performance to provide pin-point accuracy, shot to shot consistency and forgiveness when things go slightly wrong. Beyond 25 yards, though, any shaft needs extra steerage to maintain stability and accuracy and also to counteract turbulence and wind. Efficient fletchings also reduce archer error and improve the dynamic balance of front-heavy broadheads, heavyweight target and field points. They are vitally important when a bow is tuned for

Some archers consider that feathers are superior for hunting, field and short-range target shooting.

maximum speed and for ultra light, very high performance arrows like Easton aluminium/carbons.

Fletching stabilises a shaft by increasing air drag on the tail rather than by spinning it. An arrow's rotational speed bears no comparison to the high-speed stabilising spin of a bullet, but it does help reduce the effect of minor radial imbalance in the arrow – a slight bend in the shaft or uneven drag in the fletchings themselves perhaps. It also increases the steerage and drag factor, sometimes allowing a reduction in vane or feather size. Contrary to what some archers imagine, hardly any spin occurs as the arrow leaves the bow. Inertia and other factors limit the shaft to less than a tenth of a turn during this vital phase, so there are no grounds for thinking that offset or helical fletching improve arrow rest clearance.

Feathers

The outstanding advantage of feathers is their barbed structure which produces a high drag/area ratio. Drag is higher on one side of the feather, thus promoting a natural spin even if the arrow is straight fletched. These unique characteristics have been the basis of accurate shooting for thousands of years, and the most modern vanes are still inferior in certain respects.

Many hunters are convinced that feathers still provide by far the best stabilisation,

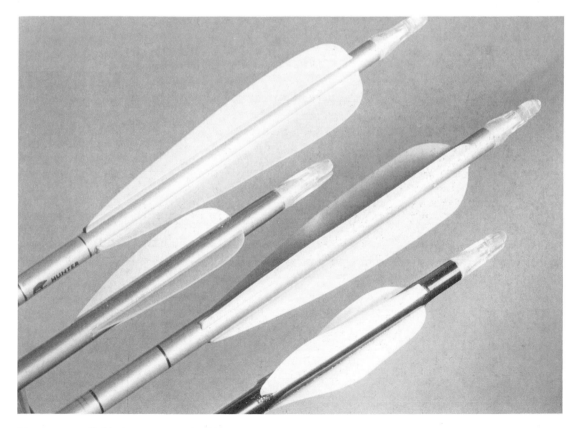

Vanes are available for every conceivable application and shaft.

steerage and forgiveness for broadheads. In the 'high-tech' atmosphere of indoor FITA target shooting, some world class archers use big feathers which kill shaft oscillations immediately after the arrow clears the bow. Good spin and pronounced drag produce a characteristically 'dead' flight which promotes pin-point accuracy and offers a little extra insurance against minor shooting errors. A few shots that would have drifted into the nine ring stay firmly in the ten.

It is generally agreed that to get the most benefit from feathers' superb performance at short range, they should be as large as possible consistent with good bow clearance. The 3–5in range covers most indoor target and hunting applications. A slight linear or helical offset is more reliable than straight fletching because it helps redress the natural drag variation between feathers. The desirable qualities of the material have been debated for thousands of years. The important points are healthy feathers ideally from the same bird or else closely matched in thickness, resilience and natural oils; a firm base quill accurately cut for precise attachment to the shaft; right wing feathers for right-handed archers, and vice versa. Old English longbowmen recommended the grey goose wing; today's archers are virtually limited to turkey – usually white because that is the most commonly bred bird.

There are serious drawbacks to feathers, however. Excellent feathers are increasingly rare, and feather fletching does not lend itself to mass production arrow building. Perfect arrow to arrow quality control is almost impossible to achieve due to natural variations in feather construction. From the practical archer's point of view they are difficult to apply, more vulnerable to damage and, even when sprayed with silicon-based water repellents, virtually impossible to protect from rain and dew.

Fletching 1 *Clean the shaft with acetone or MEK. Jig offset is 2 degrees.*

Plastic Vanes

Beyond about 50 yards, minor variations in feather fletching tend to give each arrow an individually characteristic flight pattern. If a set of arrows is 'clocked' (each shaft's individual position in the group is charted over a dozen or more shots), one arrow might fly consistently high and left, the next low and straight, and so on. Even if the group itself is fairly tight, these minor deviations are still unacceptable to high-scoring tournament archers. High quality plastic vanes are so consistent one to the next that the clocking pattern is much less noticeable or is eliminated, with arrows falling at random within the group area. If an arrow does not conform,

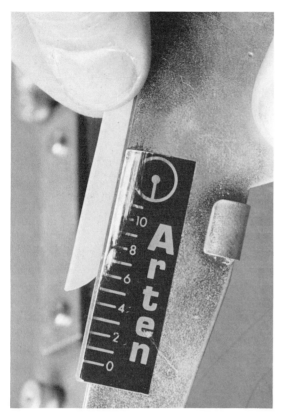

Fletching 2 *Check the vane for defects.
Clamp it, then scrub the base with acetone.*

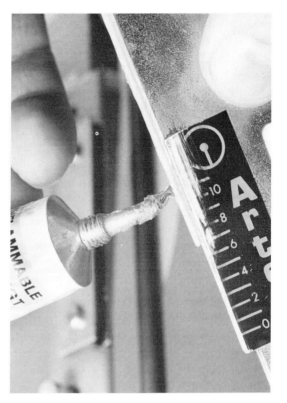

Fletching 3 *Apply an even, generous coat of adhesive.*

the cause is usually apparent – misaligned nock, unglued vane and similar damage or carelessness.

The feather's high drag factor also reduces an arrow's speed quite considerably, giving nowhere near the sight settings that can be achieved with plastic vanes. Typical sight bar improvements with 2014 shafts flying from a 42lb bow might be around half to one inch when plastic vanes and feathers are compared at 70 and 90 metres. When simplicity of application, huge freedom of choice, long life and weather resistance are added, the case for plastic vanes in tournament shooting is overwhelming. Most hunters find them perfectly acceptable as well: it is never a case of feathers good, vanes bad.

Excellent though plastic vanes are, feathers have that extra magic for some people.

Vane Selection

Vane selection is another aspect of archery where it pays to use every opportunity for improving forgiveness and reliability. Well-tuned, cleanly shot arrows are inherently stable. That being so, a small fletching will provide all the control necessary to hold a shot on perfect line right out to the longest ranges; and because the fletching imposes very little drag, arrow speed is high and sight marks are particularly good. So much for theory; in the real world of archery it is never quite so simple. Tiny vanes spell disaster for poor archers, and they never do the expert

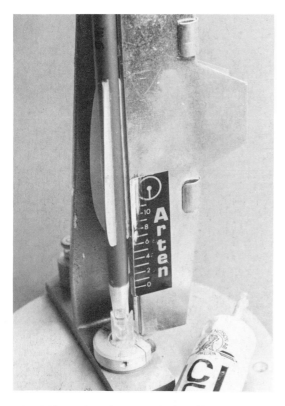

Fletching 4 *Attach vane to shaft and leave to set firmly.*

Fletching 5 *Reinforce ends of vane with an extra smear of adhesive.*

any favours either. Indeed, champions are particularly conservative in their choice of vanes or any other item; seldom, if ever, are world class archers and professional bow-hunters first to change when some new and potentially superior fletching system hits the market.

A good working formula is to fletch the shaft with the largest vane that permits clean bow clearance and comfortable sight marks at the longest distances normally shot. In combination with an inherently stable shaft of realistically high velocity and adequate weight, a target vane in the 1½–3in category to suit arrow length, weight and velocity shoots reliably and accurately under most conditions. The same goes for hunting arrows with vanes in the 3–5in range.

There is no hard evidence that any particular vane shape is best. Very low profiles are unnecessary unless bow clearance is so small that a standard vane hits the handle or rest. If so a longer, lower vane is the only way to maintain the correct drag area. Soft vanes certainly seem to present a neat solution to clearance problems, but too much flexibility results in distortion under pressure. The risk of this is minor unless vanes are awfully soft and arrow speeds excessively high, but it is one to consider particularly with cam bows, fast compounds in general and even recurves shooting aluminium/carbon arrows.

A rigid vane is more efficient for its size, does not distort at high speed, promotes better spin and generally shoots more accurately. However, stiff plastics also crack at the slightest knock and are much more difficult – in some cases impossible – to tune for clearance. Although rigid vanes are used by some extremely competent archers, most avoid them on practical grounds. Hence the popularity of semi-rigid vanes, like Plasti-fletch, which combine the best of both worlds. Modern plastics and the superior centre-shot design and tuneability of the latest tournament recurves and compounds open the door to developments. Standard profile Mylar vanes stay rigid in flight but are resilient and pliable enough to handle the occasional knock. Clearance should be no problem given the right equipment set-up, proper tuning and good style. More and more tournament archers are using these and the more specialised designs like Spinwings, which produce high spin without excessive drag or the need for pronounced offset.

NOCKS

Nocks inevitably come under the microscope when arrow performance is discussed, but in many cases where the nock itself is blamed for bad results the real villain is the swaged aluminium beneath. If the swage is accurate, nock design and fitting are relatively unimportant; quality and care are what count. Comparative tests suggest that when a nock is properly matched to the shaft and string, neatly attached and cared for, there is little difference between any of the leading brands.

Snap-on nocks are injection moulded, a process that is not only inherently accurate but also guarantees perfect continuity of performance from one batch to the next. Weight, dimensions and the characteristics of the plastic material itself are identical provided that the engineer knows his job. On the other hand, it is not only easy but actually

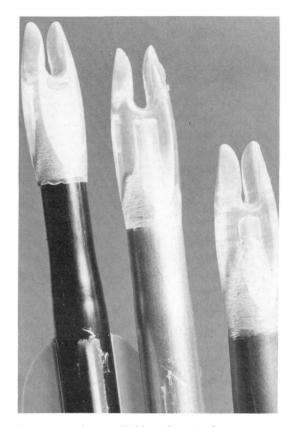

Snap-on nocks are reliable and easy to shoot.

tempting for a manufacturer to cut corners in mould design, quality control and materials specification. An inferior product looks very much like the best until you come to shoot it. Even then the deficiencies may not show up for several months – until that important tournament, or the buck of a lifetime walks under your stand.

Bjorn, Plastinock, Index, Pro Nock and similar products with an established reputation are nothing more than a commonsense choice for serious archery. They are tough, precisely tailored to the Easton swage contours and, with careful fitting, guarantee high accuracy. Sometimes the opaque shades like white and black seem a little less resistant to damage than the translucent colours, but standards are high across the range.

Fitting the Nock

Leaving aside the huge effect a badly fitted or damaged nock may have on accuracy, the real risk is to the archer himself and to anyone near him. No arrow should ever be put on a string until its nock has been checked for damage, particularly for cracks running from the swage area into the string groove. The smallest hairline crack can easily shatter under pressure with potentially dangerous results. Recurves are bad enough, but a powerful, highly tuned cam bow will literally explode the nock and send the arrow flying out of control sideways or even backwards.

The first step in fitting a nock is to match its size to that of the shaft. The angle of swaging is similar or even identical from one size of arrow to another, so there is sometimes a tendency to make do with the next nearest size or even to select it intentionally. Classic examples are where a slightly smaller nock helps prevent finger pinch or a bigger one fits the string better. Given excellent nock quality and perfect fitting, such modifications are probably both accurate and safe, but as a rule it pays to insist on the correct match because that is the only way to spread the energy input from the bow evenly across the swaged section of the arrow, thus reducing stress on shaft and nock and maintaining full performance.

Clean the swage with acetone, MEK or isopropyl alcohol, smear on a drop of adhesive, then press the nock into position. Rotate it three or four times to spread the adhesive evenly, then, as Easton themselves recommend, screw the nock back one turn to ensure perfect alignment. The nock must also be aligned with the vanes, of course. Basically, that's all there is to it: a quick, accurate, strong and reliable process.

Nock Damage

Trouble begins when a nock is damaged and must be replaced. If the swage is not already damaged by the impact (most nocks are broken because another arrow hits them), careless stripping of the broken plastic is certain to cause havoc. Hacking with a knife, cutting with pliers and any other traumatic form of nock removal is a sure way to distort the swage. The best, and probably the only, way to remove a nock safely is to soften the plastic with heat before easing it off *gently* with pliers. Rub off the old glue with cleaning agent, then apply a new nock.

Depending on how badly the swage is damaged, the choice lies between scrapping the shaft or being much more careful when the new nock is put on. Most mishaps would not have occurred if any shaft with a damaged swage was automatically thrown away, but the natural reaction is to re-nock an arrow unless it is impossible to do otherwise. Slight distortion will almost certainly affect nothing but nock life and shooting accuracy. Chunks of aluminium missing from the swage spell potential disaster, but again we tend not to discard an arrow until almost all the swage is gone. The only responsible and logical recommendation is to discard any arrow with a damaged swage; but since archers do not live in a perfectly logical world, what can be done about a damaged but still serviceable shaft?

The main problem is alignment. Clean the swage and gently file off any high spots of aluminium. Press on a dry nock. If it seats accurately on the swage, go ahead with normal gluing. If not, spread an extra amount of glue on the swage and inside the nock as well, then gently press and rotate. Ideally, check the alignment on a nock jig such as the Bjorn before leaving the adhesive to harden. After that the arrow should shoot perfectly well,

The nock must be checked every time the arrow is shot.

but it *must* be checked even more carefully between shots than an undamaged shaft. A perfect swage should not need an alignment jig provided the nock is right and only the bare minimum of the correct glue is used. On the other hand, checking never did any harm.

An intriguing new nock has appeared recently. Still something of an unknown quantity, the Beiter Super Nock dispenses with the shaft swage. Instead, it is inserted into the cut end of the shaft thus allowing – so the manufacturer claims – greater precision, strength and superior accuracy. Glance-off damage is said to be much reduced and there is no need for an alignment jig. Time will tell if they establish themselves as a serious alternative to existing designs.

The obvious drawback is that merely to test them entails cutting your precious arrows.

POINTS

The pros and cons of broadhead and target point design could fill a volume of their own. Here we are concerned with the technical aspects of accurate shooting, not penetration and killing efficiency directly. In addition, many aspects of point design are not only highly debatable but also have no bearing on target, field or hunting at any level from beginner to champion. In everyday archery, which point to use depends a great deal on personal preference or is restricted by some regulation or another. The key issue for most

9% and 7% NIBB points.

shooters is which *weight* of point to choose from the options available for the branch of archery in question. Would a 9 per cent NIBB help you shoot better scores? Which field point would be best to use for backyard practice as an alternative to the broadheads you take into the woods?

Accuracy and control are the name of the game, and the main factors involved are static balance and dynamic reaction. Static balance refers mainly to the arrow's centre of gravity. Dynamic reaction is the characteristic response of the shaft to the sudden shock when the string is released. Although the shaft itself has by far the greater influence on velocity, accuracy and KE, the point plays an important role none the less. Within the range of points designed for use with any given shaft specification, arrow length and

draw weight, one in particular usually gives the best overall result in terms of sight settings, grouping, tuneability and forgiveness.

A 9 per cent NIBB or similar heavyweight point flies in a determined sort of way, occasionally maintaining accuracy despite a noticeable amount of tail wagging. Shot into the same windy conditions, a standard arrow may appear more stable, but drifts further from the target centre. A similar pattern emerges with field points and broadheads, the latter being quite sensitive to planing at the front as well if the wind catches the blades. The risk should be small due to the short ranges and heavy shafts normally involved, but occasionally becomes prominent with very fast, light arrows shot from high poundage cam bows. Today's multi-bladed designs eliminate the inherent planing effect of traditional double-edged broadheads, so there should be no problems in that respect.

In theory, then, an arrow ought to be well weight-forward with fairly small vanes to control the back end oscillations and to provide the small degree of steerage required. As in so many aspects of archery, theory fails to hold up against the practicalities of shooting, and particularly against the often severe difficulties of maintaining accuracy and consistency in adverse conditions. The further an arrow's centre of gravity is displaced towards the front, the more unstable it becomes during the release phase.

When the string drives forward against the nock, the point and shaft of the arrow react in the classic paradox pattern. The heavier the point, the greater the inertia of the arrow, and therefore the more bending occurs. Under the shock of acceleration, a shaft's dynamic spine falls as the weight of the point increases. In simple terms, a heavier than standard point makes the shaft whippy; a lighter one forces it to react more stiffly. But the static spine (the figure given in the arrow

A second pressure button solves the tuning mismatch between broadheads and practice points.

selection matrix) remains the same whatever point is attached. Substantially lighter than normal points are rarely encountered in target shooting or hunting, so it is unlikely that an archer would ever get into trouble because the dynamic stiffness of his arrows was so high that he could not shoot them. Excessive whippiness due to heavier than standard points is extremely common; most archers run this risk at some time.

Changing from 7 per cent NIBBs to 9 per cent NIBBs involves far more than exchanging points. At the very least the bow must be retuned. Yet surprisingly few archers bother checking the nocking point, never mind the bare shaft planing pattern. To extract the advantages of the heavier point (assuming it

does have something tangible to offer, which is by no means always the case), stabilisation, string height and weight, fletching and pressure button may need to be altered. Compound peak weight and tiller must sometimes be adjusted as well, and you may also need to change the shaft's dynamic reaction, perhaps by shortening it to increase stiffness. Sometimes the shaft and point must be changed as a unit: an archer shooting 7 per cent NIBBs on 1916s might not extract the advantages of the heavier point unless he switched to 2014 shafts as well.

Similar findings emerge with broadheads and field points, but they are usually far less serious. Broadhead weights certainly do vary, but to a greater extent than in target shooting they are counteracted by the much heavier, stiffer shafts involved. Only in extreme cases will a hunting shaft fail to retune to match a heavier head. What matters more is the facility to switch between broadheads and practice points.

It is sometimes difficult to shoot broadheads and field points on the same grade shaft with equal accuracy unless the bow is tuned for each in turn. The obvious decision is to tune for hunting performance, then leave the bow alone. In all probability, the bow will shoot the same arrows fitted with field points quite accurately enough for practice provided they weigh roughly the same as the broadheads. Most points available for any given shaft specification tend to match

Shafts may look identical, but there are always a few rogues in every batch.

quite well in that respect, although problems may occur with heavier than normal broadheads that lack a field point equivalent. One solution is to choose a different arrow entirely for practice. Another is to use two interchangeable pressure buttons on the bow according to the arrow being shot. Whatever the case, some compromise is likely.

As in so many other aspects of archery, point weight selection is much more a matter of gaining a little something in performance and ease of shooting rather than a straight issue of good versus bad. Changing from standard weight target points to 9 per cent NIBBs or Klicka points will not turn a bad shooter into a champion. The extra score is merely icing on the cake unless you shoot in the rarified atmosphere of world and Olympic events where every last point counts.

CLOCKING

Modern arrows are beautifully straight, perfectly spined, and in the case of top grade target shafts, virtually 100 per cent consistent from one to the next. From the engineering point of view there is no reason why one arrow should not perform exactly the same as the others in the set; and up to quite high standards of shooting it really is impossible to find any individual variations. All the same, when scores rise beyond 1000 FITA each arrow should be checked regularly not only for straightness and integrity but for grouping pattern as well. The same applies to hunting, but this time regardless of shooting standards because a bowhunter's arrows are notoriously vulnerable to damage.

Despite the most careful nocking, fletching and maintenance, nobody can be sure of perfect results until his arrows are shot and clocked. In the old days, archers shot to discover which arrows did match; today, we

Clocking reveals defects that cannot be detected by examining the arrow itself.

aim to root out those that do not. The assumption should be that the arrow is perfectly all right until proven otherwise. A subtle observation perhaps, but one that guards against the risk of blaming the arrow for an inconsistency in control or tuning.

Wait for reasonably good conditions and shoot at the longest range at which you are confident of making good groups. Check no more than six arrows at a time, and shoot them at least a dozen times each. Record the strike pattern on diagrams representing the target face, using a separate diagram for each arrow. By building a picture of each arrow individually, you can see any deviations and inconsistencies more clearly than if all six were plotted together. Wild arrows are easy

to spot and should be examined for damage. Sometimes an arrow strays only just outside the main group, but still far enough to lose many points during a long tournament.

Be realistic about what can be gained: very few archers can shoot consistently tight, round groups. The idea is to get rid of arrows that float wide often enough not to be due to poor shooting. An obvious fault usually emerges if you look hard enough. If not, stripping and rebuilding the wayward shaft corrects what must have been a very small error in fletching or nock. Occasionally, but still more commonly than might be imagined even with premier quality arrows, the shaft or point is the real culprit and replacement is the only answer.

9 Tabs, Gloves and Release Aids

Most archers, asked which part of their technique is likely to break down under stress, blame their release without hesitation. Letting go of the string is a nightmare – the harder they try, the worse it gets. Champion archers have nothing to worry about; for them the act of letting go is a subconscious reaction, simply another step in the flow from draw to follow-through which is given no special attention. They say, 'It's something I don't even think about. It just happens.'

The release aid is often described as the perfect solution to controlling the bow string – consistent, more accurate, easier and smoother. By eliminating string torque, reducing paradox and bypassing most of the muscles in the archer's hand and forearm, it

Tab thickness should be matched to draw weight and limb performance.

is immensely valuable in target shooting and hunting. However, as discussed elsewhere, its benefits are much greater for beginners and average archers than for the champions. Any archer seriously intent on reaching the top must realise that although the release aid will probably produce slightly better accuracy than he could ever achieve with fingers, it can never replace technique and control. Dedication and talent are what makes a champion; no mechanical device will ever take their place.

TABS AND GLOVES

Clean, accurate shots from tab or glove depend on the finger muscles relaxing while the back muscles maintain full tension. The string frees itself by brushing the fingers aside, and although some friction and deflection inevitably take place, it is consistent and therefore can be minimised by tuning and bow stabilisation. A tab or shooting glove is designed to take those factors into account as well as providing a more comfortable draw, anchor and hold.

A good tab is thick enough to prevent the string cutting into the fingers, but flexible enough not to hold a crease which interferes with release. A single thickness of leather is enough for bows less than 30lb, but higher weights need extra cushioning. Rather than increase the leather thickness directly, it is much better to use a tough face lined with an inner tab of softer leather. When the string moves forward, the two layers slide against each other to produce a clean, smooth action.

Within reason, a tab should extend no further along the fingers than is strictly necessary for protection, but it should be deep enough to give a generous overwrap to the bottom of the third finger. Many archers suffer pain and callouses here which they

blame on release pressure. Although string scrubbing certainly makes a contribution, nipping at full draw due to the angle of the string is at least as much to blame. If the finger does get scrubbed, the likely reason is excess tension in the little finger which prevents the third finger from relaxing.

Excessive friction between the first and second fingers usually indicates a fault in technique. The fingers are not spaced properly either side of the arrow nock, and there is probably unwanted tension in the back of the hand as well. However, high draw weights sometimes force the fingers too close together, giving rise to high friction and interference with the nock's escape. Fitting a spacer block to the tab and making sure that the draw hand stays relaxed usually solves this problem.

Top archers are not agreed on the value of an anchor platform. Some insist that an accurate anchor depends at least as much on tactile sense as on mechanical positioning. They do not feel fully in control unless the index finger actually touches the face. However, since there are excellent archers in both camps, this is probably another example of personal preference being the deciding factor. A real advantage of the platform is that it usually lowers the draw hand position enough to make long-range shooting more comfortable due to the improved sight plane. It ensures much more accurate vertical alignment for archers who use a pronounced side-of-face anchor.

The shooting glove follows much the same principles as the tab, but seldom gives the same accuracy. To make up for that, it is more convenient, comfortable and quicker to use in hunting. Within reason, the leather inserts sewn into the glove fingers should be as thin and flexible as possible consistent with the bow's draw weight. Short hunting bows have a tendency to pinch the fingers as

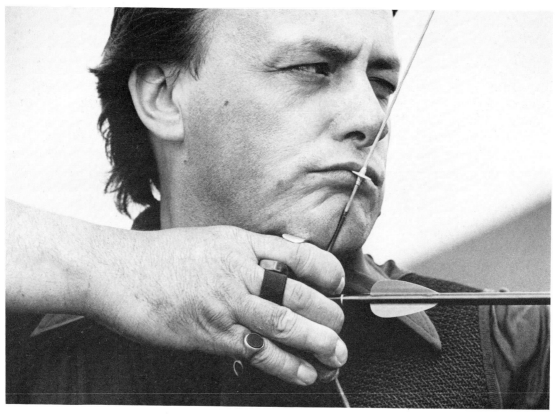

Comfort, control and precise anchor alignment are key factors in tab design.

well, so a good wrap-around on the index and third finger is essential.

Materials and Lubricants

Pony butt leather is by far the most durable material for tabs and glove inserts. Since the days of the English longbow, nothing has surpassed it. With proper dressing and care, it is at least as accurate as other faces although it gives a slower release than slippery synthetics or hair. Low friction materials like hair and plastic may increase arrow speed and conceivably give a shade more accuracy, but they wear quickly and therefore cannot be as consistent in the long term.

High quality pony butt lasts for at least a year's hard tournament shooting and, if anything, improves with age and use given proper dressing and lubrication. Saddle soap is reasonably good, but for the best results use neat's-foot oil, also available from saddlers and equestrian suppliers. When deeply impregnated, the tab is waterproof, pliable and moderately fast. No powder or extra lubricant on the bow string should be necessary.

RELEASE AIDS

From the purely mechanical point of view, a release aid ensures a cleaner, quicker freeing of the bow string that fingers could never match. It is generally agreed that the ideal

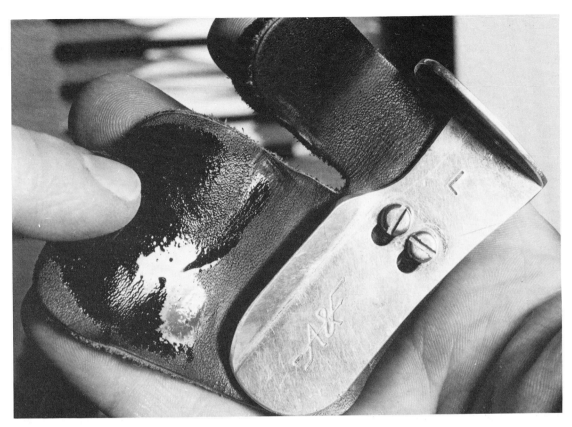

Neat's-foot oil soaks into leather, making it supple, waterproof and durable.

circumstances for perfect release aid function is when the archer is at full draw with the weight held on his back, pulling hard against the stops and aiming intently. According to his style, he then concentrates on maintaining the hold or increasing his back tension while squeezing the trigger until the shot breaks. Only under those conditions can the release operate efficiently and maximum accuracy be expected.

More than anything, the ideal aid is the one that does not interfere with the archer's style. It should be comfortable to hold, easy to operate, consistent, adjustable for trigger pressure and travel, and safe. Most high quality aids conform to those requirements, so the only way to narrow the field down to

one model in particular is by testing the options available. On paper some designs offer distinct advantages, but there is no real evidence that, say, little finger operation is better than thumb release; that holding the release with three fingers is necessarily less accurate than a wrist or palm hold; that two-stage mechanisms are better than a plain sear. Fashions change, innovations come and go, and advertising adds more fuel to the fire. Try them all, then pick the one that feels right and shoots reliably; that is what the champions do.

Release Triggering

Tension and torque in the draw hand some-times make little finger operation difficult or even impossible. When the bow is at full draw and on aim, the archer subconsciously tenses and twists his hand so badly that the finger muscles freeze. Only a small amount of that tension is transmitted to the bow string if a rope-type aid is used, but in hunting with a direct attachment system, the result could be high friction, violent paradox reaction, erratic KE output and bad grouping. Because the little finger is usually sympathetically linked to the third finger (if the third is tense, the little finger will be equally affected although it is not directly involved in drawing the bow), it is also very difficult to achieve the smooth squeeze so essential for good shooting. Triggering becomes a snatchy affair, involving a drop in back tension as well. Even with a cushion of rope around the string, the shot is ragged.

The obvious answer is to reduce muscle tension, but if that is impossible – which it may be if the archer has been shooting that way for many years – a thumb or third finger trigger makes life easier. The third finger is seldom strongly sympathetic with the first and second fingers that draw the bow, so it

Correct release aid technique demonstrated by Master Bowman Philip van Buren. Properly set up and on aim, Philip concentrates on back tension while squeezing the trigger.

does not generate so much snatch and torque. The obvious snag is that draw weight is now confined to just two fingers.

The thumb is usually unaffected by finger tension, so it is particularly adept at squeezing a trigger. Overall, the thumb-activated release aid feels comfortable, precise and secure, and is therefore by far the best option for many target archers and is popular for hunting as well. Spreading the draw weight evenly across the hand, it is an excellent choice for heavy bows.

Finger-style recurve archers who prefer to shoot the compound with a release aid – during hunting season, for example – some- times do better with thumb release even though there is no tension in their fingers. Squeezing with the third or even the little finger feels wrong; moreover, they are nervous about developing any reflexes that may interfere with their finger release. A tiny minority of archers taught to shoot traditionally with tab or glove suffer a much more dramatic problem with finger-operated releases: they occasionally let go of the whole release aid instead of triggering the mechanism.

The pressure and control continue unbroken until after the arrow escapes.

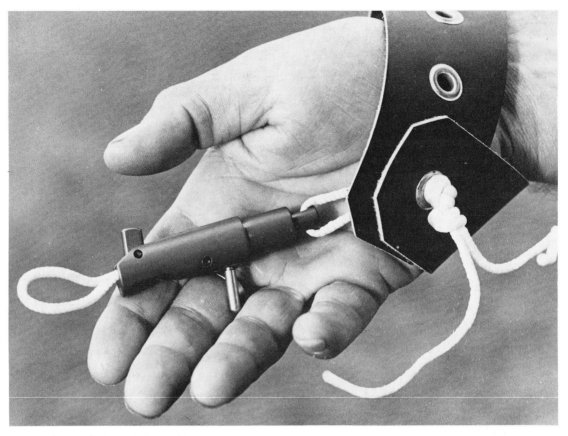

Fletchmatic wrist release with index finger triggering.

Wrist and Palm Hold

Unwanted tension in the fingers and back of the hand is neatly bypassed with a release attached to the wrist or held in the palm. Wrist attachment along with complete relaxation of the draw forearm not only eliminates unwanted pressures around the hand but also virtually guarantees that the back muscles operate reasonably well at least. However, full back tension does not develop automatically with the use of a wrist release. Given the low holding weight of a compound bow, it is still possible to draw and hold with the upper arm and shoulder muscles predominantly. The palm release operates in a similar manner by shifting the draw arm fulcrum from the finger joints to the wrist. Provided the wrist itself stays relaxed at full draw, unwanted tensions and torque are much reduced.

Palm and wrist releases leave the index finger free to operate the trigger. This is a very positive system for archers already familiar with firearms. Pulling with the back while squeezing the trigger with the index finger has obvious parallels with rifle shooting, and in addition generates a comfortable line of pressure through the draw elbow which in turn helps concentrate the archer's mind on back tension and maintained follow-through.

Rope or Direct Attachment

The rope release dominates target archery because it is more consistent and accurate. The rope absorbs quite a lot of torque from the bow wrist without affecting the string; paradox and tuning are more controllable because the rope imposes very little friction when the string accelerates. The loop should be long enough to let the archer rotate his hand and forearm at full draw (most archers find it much more natural and comfortable to shoot when the palm faces away from the face) but not so long that it interferes with the string's path. Inconsistent release may occur if the rope goes clockwise around the bow string. For maximum accuracy and minimum shaft oscillation it should wrap around the string in the same direction that fingers would.

Locking the release aid directly on to the string is a much more practical system for hunting. However, the disadvantages of this are that release is harsher and noisier due to the extra friction between jaws and serving, and offers much less cushioning against draw arm tensions. Even if the jaws are housed in a swivelling block, torque can still be a problem. Attaching the release directly to the bow inevitably means that the metal locking mechanism wears away the string serving, but this is usually of no consequence considering how few arrows are shot.

Trigger Adjustment

Just as rifle and pistol shooters find that a very light trigger creates problems unless every other area of technique is nearly perfect, so highly sensitive release aids are a menace for all but the best of archers. Significantly, most leading tournament archers who could use a hair trigger prefer not to do so. Release aids adjusted for moderate pressure and medium travel are of great assistance when the archer is under stress. They are the commonsense choice for the majority of target shooters and hunters of all standards, not least from the safety angle. If the release goes off when little more than finger weight is applied, the archer often develops a nervous twitch of the operating finger or thumb; basically he is scared to touch the lever. Similarly, without a detectable amount of free travel before the mechanism trips, the tendency is to freeze rather than squeeze.

Pressure of 2–3lb and $\frac{1}{8}$in of travel are a good basis for experiment, and above all they

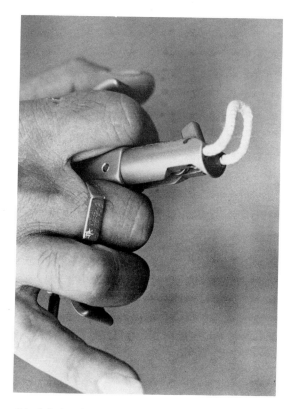

Ideal design for target shooting: bow pressure is spread over three fingers, and the little finger triggers the lever. The rope gives a clean, fast release with minimum paradox.

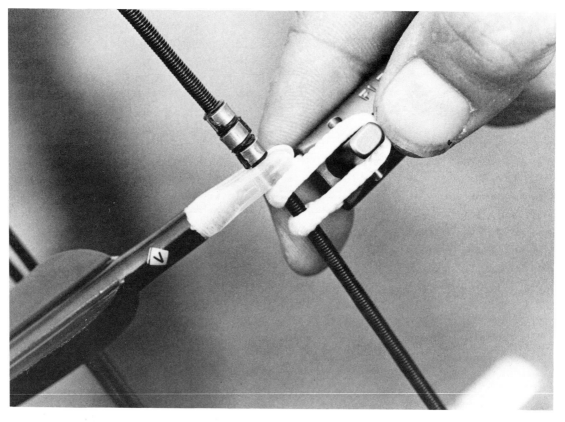

Safety must never be compromised. An over-sensitive release aid is potentially dangerous – and may well be less accurate.

reduce the chances of accidental release such as all too often occurs when the archer inadvertently touches an oversensitive trigger half-way through the draw. Even higher pressure may be necessary to prevent premature release due to nervousness. Again, this reflects what firearms shooters have known for years: oversensitive trigger mechanisms are more trouble than they are worth, even for experts.

10 Sighting

Accurate aiming comprises three distinct areas of control and precision:

1. Basic alignment of the bow's force lines with the archer's skeleton and muscles.
2. Preliminary alignment of this body/bow unit with the target.
3. Precise visual alignment of sight pin and aiming spot.

This interplay of style, control and eye is a fundamental building block of accurate shooting, but it is usually ignored because most archers think of aiming only in the visual sense.

Confusion about aiming stems from the apparently logical parallels between archery and rifle shooting. The newcomer to archery assumes that if he can aim a rifle – which the majority of people can do fairly well without any difficulty – he can aim a bow just as accurately because the principles are exactly the same; the only real difference is that the rear sight becomes an anchor point. Unfortunately, he ignores that fluid relationship between archer, bow and arrow.

The Barrel

The sights of a firearm have a permanent relationship with the barrel. As the sights are lined up with the target, the barrel automatically follows. When the trigger is squeezed, the bullet is discharged along the right line at predictable velocity and trajectory due to the precise amount of powder in the cartridge. Once a firearm has been sighted in, accuracy and grouping are directly linked to how precisely the shooter aims and holds. Firearm

and ammunition quality, trigger control and general competence are limiting factors, of course, but there remains the basic relationship between sighting and shot. The better you aim, the tighter the group will be.

The 'barrel' of a bow – that is, the straightness of shot – is affected by a list of variables including hand placement on the grip, fingers on the string, how accurately the body is aligned with bow and target, anchor point and string picture. Not only can the 'barrel' form a different relationship with the sights from one shot to the next, sometimes it is 'bent' due to excessive bow hand torque, tilting limb or anything else that sends the arrow off to one side. To make matters worse, the 'powder charge' can vary considerably due to variations in draw length, back tension, release control and follow-through. Thus, trajectory can also change substantially from one shot to the next. Aiming in the visual sense therefore becomes an unpredictable business because the arrow's energy and direction are not consistently aligned with the sights. Although the sight pin is held exactly in the ten ring, the arrow could still miss the face entirely.

Two Stage Process

Aiming in archery is a two stage process. First the body/bow/arrow unit must be correctly prepared to ensure consistent line and power in the shot and also to establish a sound relationship between the archer himself and the target. In practice, this means setting up the shot as well as possible from preparation to draw, anchor, hold and eventually to release and follow-through – in

Archers aim by bringing body, bow, sight and target into common alignment by a two stage process.

other words technique and control. Strict attention to detail ensures that the fully drawn arrow is correctly aligned with the sight and will be released from a stable platform with consistent energy.

Experts describe the visual stage of sighting which follows as little more than confirmation of what they already knew: that body, bow and arrow lie in their proper relationship to the target. Fine tuning of the sight picture certainly contributes considerably towards better groups and higher scores, but it is equally important as a source of confidence and as a focal point for their concentration. Ninety per cent of aiming has already been taken care of during the setting up of the shot due to stance and upper body

alignment, so in most cases nothing more than minor adjustments are necessary to stabilise the pin in the centre of the gold.

SIGHTING PRINCIPLES

Archery can be amazingly accurate without mechanical sights, as bare bow events prove. The champion shoots groups almost as tight as the best recurve target archers can hope to achieve: sighting along the arrow for direction; using gap estimation, string walking or face walking methods to control elevation, depending on the regulations. The truly instinctive archer uses no conscious control, yet still shoots very well. Though he may not

Long extensions should be treated with caution.

realise it, he actually uses a combination of man's innate talent for pointing, reinforced by a mental image derived from the position of the bow, size of target and other visual references, most of them at subconscious level. In every case, basic alignment and consistency during the shot's physical execution create and maintain the framework for success.

A mechanical sight always has the advantage over bare bow techniques, so at the highest levels of the sport the freestyle archer inevitably comes out on top. An unfortunate spin-off is that less able freestyle and FITA archers assume that a sight is absolutely essential for shooting even moderately well, which obviously it is not. They develop far too much reliance on the sight picture and

nowhere near enough on the physical controls.

Comparing champions to less able archers, it is difficult to detect much difference in visual aiming skills. The glaring disparity is in the setting up of the shot, a stage of aiming that many archers fail to recognise, never mind to control and develop. Without a fair degree of competence there, visual aiming is a wasted effort. Why concentrate on a perfect sight picture if the arrow could land anywhere in a 48in circle? The concept is not only invalid but also creates serious problems: every time he misses, the archer concentrates even more on the visual side of aiming. The harder he tries to hold the sight steady in the gold, the more tense he becomes, and in turn the worse he shoots

An open ring reduces tension and improves the archer's control.

until eventually his control breaks down completely.

All except a few champions are plagued by this hidden conflict between physical and visual accuracy, which is another way of saying that 99 per cent of archers over-aim and under-shoot. Intriguing concepts can be deduced from that situation. What happens if the archer shifts his concentration from visual aiming, and instead pays much more attention to technique and control? What is the difference in group diameter and scoring power between strong, consistent shots aimed approximately at the middle of the target, and weak, inconsistent shots aimed exactly at the middle of the ten ring? In virtually every case, shifting the emphasis from sight picture to control gives much

tighter groups and significantly higher scores.

When an archer puts together an excellent shot – call it a 'ten' – even if the sight is in the red when he lets go, the worst he scores is a seven. Conversely, why bother sweating to keep the pin in the gold when poorly controlled arrows fly from the bow as threes, ones or complete misses? There are other factors involved also. Good, strong shots often develop an accuracy of their own, so that even when the sight is wavering in the red/gold area, a disproportionate number of arrows still hit the gold; the group is actually tighter than the sight picture suggests. Logically this is impossible, but presumably due to subconscious corrections of some kind, it does happen. Sometimes when an excellent archer is really on form, the arrow still goes in the gold although he swears the pin was on the edge of the blue when he released.

Follow-through

A more relaxed approach to sighting generally does nothing but good for technique, confidence and scores. There is a slight risk, however, that paying too little attention to the sight picture could cause serious damage to the follow-through. Without exception, top class archers stress the need to 'keep pressing the sight into the gold', 'hold the aim until the arrow strikes' or similar. In hunting, the advice is to 'pick a hair and concentrate on it.'

At the highest level of shooting, there can be no compromise on sight picture. Sight pin and anchor point are precisely controlled, and the archer makes a conscious effort to aim at the very centre of the ten ring. He can afford to do so because his form, control and confidence are of an extraordinary standard. But the sight picture has another important function: it is the focal point for the archer's concentration. By staring intently at the pin or the gold or the hair behind a deer's shoulder, he virtually hypnotises himself into maintaining total control of the shot, no aspect of which is more critical than follow-through.

Archers of lower standard should therefore appreciate the difference between under-aiming and lack of concentration. Allowing the sight pin to drift a little more generously than before does not mean losing concentration on the target itself. If anything, this should be increased. For most people the trick is to focus the eye on the target while the blurred sight pin hovers somewhere near the middle, then maintain visual concentration on the target until the arrow strikes. If this is given priority, the

mechanical side of the follow-through is much more likely to develop along the right lines. When champions speak of mental control being at least as important as physical skill, this is one area to which they refer.

CHOOSING A SIGHT

The key features of a sight for target shooting and hunting are broadly the same: precise adjustments for windage and elevation over the required ranges, settings that stay put, no interference with the arrow and dependable construction. In purely objective terms, it is questionable whether the most sophisticated of sights, complete with carbonfibre extension and micrometer scales, gives a significantly more accurate aiming picture than a dressmaker's pin stuck to the bow with Scotch tape, assuming that each is properly adjusted. Of course, there is much more to it than that, but it never hurts to bear in mind the underlying imbalance between how well an archer can aim compared to his much lower ability to shoot consistently accurate groups. Owing to the tensions and frustrations of over-aiming, some archers who switch to very advanced sights – telescopic foresights especially – end up shooting much worse than before.

Nobody would suggest a return to pin-and-tape sights as a means of improving shooting standards, but there is much to be gained from a simple approach. Investment in a top quality sight generally repays itself many times in durability, ease of adjustment, availability of spares and, above all, freedom to alter extension, ring diameter and sight elements. Although little is gained in pure aiming precision by such fine-tuning, there is a tremendous psychological boost in shooting with a customised sight picture that looks and feels right.

A top quality sight lasts longer and can be altered to produce the preferred aiming picture. However, a much cheaper sight can be equally accurate.

Sight Extension

Extending the sight ring from the bow produces a sharper picture which, depending on the individual's eyesight, may allow both the element and the target face to be in focus at the same time. The extra clarity usually increases confidence and may even solve the eternal question of whether to focus on the target or the sight. World class archers dispute which plane of focus is better, though all are agreed that the eye should never be allowed to drift back and forth. If it does, concentration automatically wavers as well.

Increasing the distance between the element and the anchor point also increases the sight's sensitivity, which is not only unneces-sary for the vast majority of archers but also exaggerates the slightest movements of bow and body. In extreme cases, the sight element dances across the target face, aiming becomes more frustrating, tension develops and the classic results of over-aiming inevit-ably follow. Although the expert archer may find some benefit in an extension bar about a foot long, 4–6in is as much as most archers can handle. Even then they may find it hard to live with the extra wobble on windy days.

Excessive extension sometimes throws the bow out of balance. The track and sight block of heavy sights like the Chek-it become an additional stabiliser if the extension bar is longer than 6in. As well as altering the bow's in-hand balance and release reaction, they

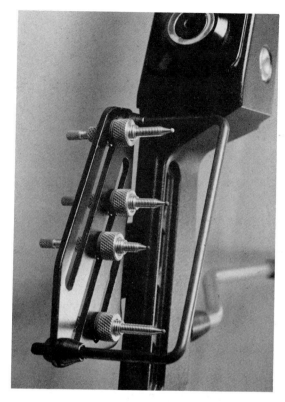

Barnett's multi-pin hunting sight. Each pin is independently adjustable for windage and elevation.

may affect the tuning as well. All this can be allowed for if extension remains constant and the bow is set up and tuned accordingly, but may cause problems if the extension is altered for various distances – typically, lengthened at the shorter FITA ranges. The best solution is a modern sight like the Yamaha YS–V or Arten Olympic with a non-extending track that concentrates the weight close to the bow handle.

Rings and Elements

Small rings and delicate elements often ruin smooth execution of the shot by absorbing too much of the archer's concentration. The smaller the pin, crosshair or ring, the greater

the urge to fight for absolute stability and alignment. Almost without exception, archers suffering from over-aiming are cured by a switch to a fairly large open ring. Concentration shifts back to technique and control, arrows fly more cleanly and consistently, and despite that big, clumsy ring the groups are tight and central.

The open ring is successful for several reasons. It relaxes the archer, who then shoots better. It also brings into play another of man's natural talents: he is extremely good at aligning rings to be concentric with each other, and at placing an object in the centre of a circle. Laboratory tests produce fascinating data, some of it opposite to what one might assume. Of direct value to shooters in general and archers in particular is the fact that precision of alignment is not directly related to the comparative diameters of the rings, nor to the size of a target object compared to the aperture. Most people can place a penny in the middle of a 12in circle as accurately as in 3in; or align a distant target as precisely in a 2in ring as in an aperture less than a quarter that diameter.

This natural ability explains why some archers can aim through a ring sight so big that at 90 metres the whole target face sits inside with room to spare, yet still shoot groups in the red/gold. Some align the ring with the central dot of the gold itself; others adjust the sight ring to be concentric with the coloured rings in general. With only a little experience, the process becomes almost entirely subconscious, controlled by this strange power we all possess.

None of this is news to rifle and pistol shooters who have known for decades that target and foresight will automatically fall into alignment with the exact centre of the rear sight aperture. They are also slightly dubious about the archer's choice of aiming spot on the target face itself. The aiming spot

Simple but accurate and reliable: the Arten Summit bow sight.

in rifle and pistol shooting is always much bigger than the highest scoring ring. To hit a ¾in bull at about 25 yards, the pistol shooter would aim at a spot about 3in across. It makes no difference that he cannot even see the ten ring. Yet the experts would consistently hit the X-ring, which is inside the ten ring itself. At similar distances on smaller targets, but still with an aiming spot considerably bigger than the inner X, smallbore riflemen shoot so accurately that a separate target is used for each shot. Together, ten shots would produce a group no bigger than a single arrow hole.

The same principle is used outdoors, even at ranges beyond half a mile. The picture seen through the sights is always similar: a generous aiming spot sitting above an equally broad foresight element. Somehow this approach does not equate with archery, but, considering how much better most archers do shoot by taking a more relaxed attitude, perhaps there is scope for serious investigation of sighting principles in general. The immediate conclusion is that inexperienced archers at least should be wary of crosshairs and similar delicate elements intended to increase visual sensitivity but which actually produce lower scores. It is surely not a coincidence that so many top class archers use fairly large, plain rings with or without a simple pin.

Adjustments

Nothing is more annoying than a sight block that vibrates loose or slips out of adjustment. High quality construction, a toothed track with lockable worm gear and micrometer screws are highly desirable for target shooting. Once calibrated, a hunting sight is unlikely to be altered as often, so there is no need for such complex adjustments. Locking nuts on the windage screw and firm bolts to hold the pins in the vertical slide-ways are an accurate and durable system found on the majority of multipin sights.

Adjustment of the track itself is very important for target shooting because the sight block must run up and down parallel with the bow string. Otherwise the shots will drift to one side when the elevation is changed, which is not only highly disconcerting but also makes deliberate windage alterations more difficult to calculate. Usually the track can be set accurately enough by eye, but for perfect results use a spirit level. Multipin hunting sights normally have no facility to alter the tracking; instead, the pins are individually calibrated for windage.

Occasionally it is necessary to offset the whole sight away from the window to prevent arrows hitting the track and sight block, or to give enough windage compensation for a left-to-right wind. The risk is highest when

Release aid, peep and 'scope enhance the compound's performance only if the archer himself is good enough to exploit them.

the arrow is set close to centre-shot and the paradox oscillations are quite pronounced. A few models have enough sideways adjustment on the track and extension bar to create space for the arrow, but more likely the mounting plate must be packed out. Shifting the track and block inevitably means that the sight pin must be screwed out to compensate. If there is not enough adjustment left in reserve to cope with a right-to-left wind, exchange the standard pin for one with a longer bolt. The longest currently available is on the Arten Olympic, which being of standard thread can be fitted to most other popular sights. Arrows fouling the sight is quite a common problem and sometimes

difficult to detect. A coat of talcum powder on the shaft reveals the tell-tale signs.

COMPOUND BOWS

One of the biggest advantages of the compound is its let-off at full draw. Coupled to the bow's compact, nicely balanced design, this leads to greater steadiness and control especially towards the end of a long tournament. Provided the archer draws and holds with his back and shoulder muscles, a release aid adds that final touch of expertise. Hunters appreciate the compound bow for similar reasons of control and accuracy, plus the

Telescopic sights with aiming spot and spirit level are available in a range of powers.

ability to handle much higher draw weights than they could manage on a recurve bow.

Peep and 'Scope

String peep, spirit level and 'scope foresight are a natural result of the quest for 100 per cent performance from bow and arrow. Although many experienced archers use this system successfully, there are serious problems in store for the less competent archer who does not understand the limitations as well as the benefits of changing from a plain ring or pin and a conventional anchor. It is immediately obvious to anyone who studies unlimited competitors that the overwhelming majority suffer from acute over-aiming. Lining up the peep sight and spirit level is problem enough. Struggling to align the aiming dot with the magnified image of a gold that dances in and out of the 'scope is just impossible. The weight of the bow comes off the back and on to the arms, the release explodes uncontrollably, and the arrow flirts anywhere.

Extremely good archers who can master a peep and 'scope probably do gain something in accuracy, though it is probably much more a matter of confidence and personal preference than enhanced aiming precision. Judged by Olympic rifle and pistol disciplines and even recurve archery, there is no clear-cut reason why a telescopic sight should be of particular benefit. No doubt the subject could be argued forever, with logic on both sides. The important point is that these sophisticated sights should be approached with a great deal of care and consideration. They are not absolutely essential and in many cases are frankly undesirable.

Successful use of the 'scope is absolutely dependent on the archer's form and control, since if he cannot guarantee making perfect

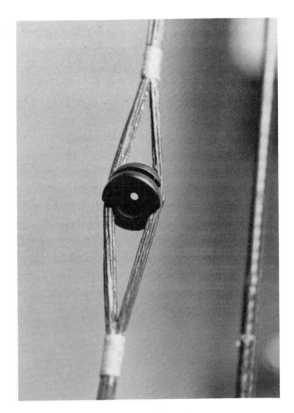

A tiny hole in the peep seldom gives more accuracy, but always reduces the light.

shots not only is the sight wasted but will certainly lead to a breakdown in whatever skill he does have. The consensus among expert compound shooters is that beginners and inexperienced archers should stick to conventional sights until they reach a high standard. Even then, a 'scope should be introduced with care, preferably under the supervision of a coach. Low power magnification is essential at this stage: the sight picture wobble will be less disconcerting and it will be easier to align the dot on the gold. On some high power 'scopes, the angle of view is so narrow that it is difficult to locate the target in the first place.

String peeps are unlikely to destroy an archer's form, but they do need careful thought. The main risks, apart from the ever

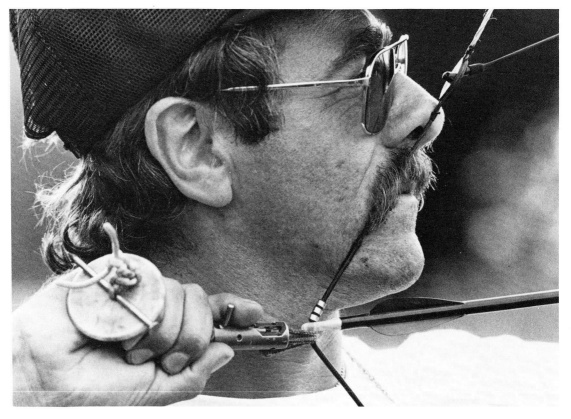

Peep sights are not an alternative to anchoring. The string must still contact the face.

present encouragement to over-aim, are loss of anchor and failure to properly set up and hold the shot itself. A common mistake is to draw back the bow, then move the head – and if necessary the arms and shoulders as well – until the eye, peep and sight dot are aligned. The theory here is that once these reference points are correctly lined up, the shot must be accurate. This ignores the crucially important relationship between draw force lines, body alignment and controlled release and follow-through – subjects discussed earlier in the chapter. The proper technique is to concentrate on building up the draw, anchor and hold, which themselves should bring the peep and the 'scope into correct alignment with the eye. At most,

only a small corrective movement of the head should be allowed.

The string peep enhances and refines the traditional face reference points, but it is no alternative to anchoring. Release aid users, and sometimes finger shooters as well, often forget how much stability and back-end control the anchor provides in addition to its other role as a rear sight. The peep should therefore be inserted into the string after the anchor position is firmly established. The only drawback is that some archers find difficulty in reaching the 90-metre FITA distance with the fairly high side-of-face anchor commonly used with a release aid. In this case, it is more sensible to raise the peep than to reduce the front sight extension (for optical reasons, a scope is almost impossible to use inside the bow handle). First a new anchor point should be established lower on the face, then the peep should be adjusted to it.

A fairly minor point concerns peep diameter. There is very little accuracy to be gained by reducing the size of the hole due to the limited space between eye and peep. The circle of vision hardly changes unless the hole diameter is huge or miniscule; the depth of field (the optical phenomenon that produces a clear image of the gold in the scope) is little different either. All that really happens is that small peeps seriously reduce brightness and clarity. As a rule, choose a diameter appropriate to the ambient light level.

Appendix: Tuning Matched Equipment

An understanding of equipment performance and matching automatically takes care of basic set-up. With this completed, the archer's next job is to familiarise himself with the particular quirks and characteristics of his outfit. Brace height, string specification and stabiliser balance/reaction must be determined on a trial and error basis. As the outfit is already inherently stable, the process will be straightforward and the results will speak for themselves. One particular combination of settings will produce the greatest smoothness, cleanliness of launch and forgiveness. Grouping will improve as well.

Fine tuning is then a simple process of checking and if necessary correcting the arrow's tendency to fishtail and porpoise (sideways and vertical deviation respectively). Nocking point and tillering take care of the latter, while button pressure, centre-shot and poundage control the former. The two patterns are interrelated, though, so altering one may affect the other. Rebalance as necessary until the arrow flies properly.

The aim of tuning is to bring all alignments, balance points and forces involved into such harmony that the arrow leaves the bow cleanly and with minimum paradox oscillation. Under those conditions a bow shoots most accurately, predictably and with the maximum stability and forgiveness. The various tuning tests available are based on those principles. All they do is measure the unwanted pressures that divert the arrow from its intended course. Most archers are already familiar with the full details of these

procedures, but for those who are not the excellent book *Bow Tuning* by Roy Matthews MBE (available from Marksman and other British archery dealers) is packed with step-by-step instructions.

Shooting an arrow or bare shaft into the boss from about six feet gives a good reflection of the arrow's stability as it leaves the bow. Nock high or low, left or right indicates a fault which later in the arrow's flight would show up as porpoising, fishtailing or a combination of the two. Although the test is fast becoming obsolete, it is perfectly good enough for fine tuning provided that the basic set-up is correct. Under those conditions, tuning the arrow so that it impacts with the shaft pointing straight back at the archer is often enough to guarantee perfect results.

The shaft planing test entails shooting bare and fletched shafts at 15–20 yards. Matched, tuned equipment produces a single group. Otherwise, the bare shaft deviates away from the fletched arrows, its position being diagnostic. High or low means nocking point misalignment. Left or right indicates that the arrow is reacting stiff or soft for some reason: it could be the wrong shaft, bad centre shot adjustment, incorrect poundage on a compound bow, button pressure, brace height or even stabilisation.

As an extension of the planing test, the walk-back system assesses minor variations of the fishtailing pattern. Essentially developed to differentiate between button pressure and centre-shot alignment, it reveals the flight characteristics of the arrow at

5-yard intervals over a 30-yard span beginning 5 yards away from the target. An aiming point at the top of the target is used and the sight is not adjusted between ranges, thus spreading the shots down the target. Ideally, the arrows should impact vertically beneath each other as the archer walks back. According to whether it is angled left or right, and either straight or curved, an imaginary line connecting the shafts reveals exactly where the fault lies.

There is no consensus among the top archers as to which of the tuning systems is best. Some use the planing test only; others the planing test for nocking height, then the walk-back for the button. A surprisingly large number of excellent archers, including some of the champions, rely on the old six-foot impact test. In their view, if the arrow comes out of the bow nice and straight, that is all they need to know.

Ultimately though, all are agreed that the only proof of good tuning is a tight group. No matter what the various tests indicate, they will usually run a few experiments with brace height, centre-shot and stabilisers to see the effect on a group at 50 metres or more. New settings that bring the arrows closer to each other are retained regardless of any changes that may occur in the bare shaft or walk-back pattern. Taking that theory to its ultimate conclusion, an archer may do all his tuning simply by shooting groups on a trial and error basis. A few also observe the arrow's flight. They can see where the fault lies by the way the shaft flickers and deviates. But in every case, everyone stresses that equipment matching and set-up must be right in the first place. Which, if you recall the Introduction, is where we came in.